The Essential **Mexican Instant Pot**® Cookbook

The Essential Mexican Instant Pot® Cookbook

Authentic Flavors and Modern Recipes for Your Electric Pressure Cooker

DEBORAH SCHNEIDER

Photography by ERIN SCOTT

TEN SPEED PRESS
California | New York

Contents

INTRODUCTION

In this book, it is my great pleasure to bring one of the world's oldest cuisines to the modern cooking system that has already transformed home cooking: the Instant Pot.

Whether you're new to Mexican cooking or looking for your favorite dishes, in each chapter you'll find authentic Mexican recipes made using traditional ingredients, with techniques and methods adapted to make the best use of the Instant Pot.

The stars of authentic Mexican cooking are slow-cooked braises and stews, which form the basis for many other dishes, from tacos to tamales to burritos. The Instant Pot dramatically speeds up the cooking process, transforming what used to take hours of work into delicious results in less than an hour.

Another frequently used technique in Mexican cooking is quick, high-heat reduction to intensify flavors. The Instant Pot will fry, simmer, and reduce—and even make refried beans. It takes the guesswork out of tamales and cuts the cooking time in half. And the essential Mexican salsas come together in mere minutes. These are just a few of the ways the Instant Pot will bring great Mexican food to your table.

Even with forty-plus years of professional cooking experience, I find the possibilities of the Instant Pot exciting and eye-opening. I quickly became proficient at using my Instant Pots, which now have a permanent spot on my kitchen counter. I would take them to a desert island (hopefully, a lush tropical one, with lots of chiles).

The Instant Pot is the perfect convenience for people who live in the fast lane. Instead of relying on convenience foods, which really don't save time (and are made with who-knows-what), in minutes you can create a healthful, delicious Mexican meal made with quality ingredients that *you* control. With a little planning, you can keep your freezer stocked with the basics for a feast: broths, sauces and salsas, beans and soups, and savory main dishes.

The Instant Pot is remarkably versatile and fast—with delicious results. Use it to make soups, beans, and stews; cook rice and vegetables; steam tamales; and even bake cakes. It serves as a warming unit (which comes in handy if your family eats at different times) or a buffet server, and it's smart enough to cook a dish for the correct amount of time and then keep it warm until you are ready to sit down for dinner.

Once you learn the different features of your Instant Pot, cooking will be so much easier. The pot's preprogrammed functions and timer mind the cooking for you. No need to fuss over settings or adjust burners. Just press a few buttons and go!

So let's fire it up and make something amazing!

- Deb

Getting to Know the Instant Pot

The simple tips below will help you get acquainted with your Instant Pot and determine how best to use it for your needs.

Read the manual. Read your manual to familiarize yourself with the assembly, function keys, indicator lights, and the operation of the lid and steam release handle on your particular model. Put it together and take it apart a few times so you are confident handling the parts, especially setting and locking the lid and moving the steam release handle.

Cook safely. Read all safety instructions in the user's manual. The Instant Pot builds pressure at a high temperature, so knowing how to safely release the hot steam and remove the lid is essential. The contents will also be extremely hot. Always err on the side of caution and allow the contents to both release all steam and cool slightly before handling. Use protective oven mitts or thick kitchen towels when grasping the hot inner pot. Never fill the inner pot more than two-thirds full with liquid or food.

Try it out. Choose a few simple recipes, such as Arroz Blanco (page 134) or Cowboy Pinto Beans (page 129), and put it through its paces. After using it a couple of times, you will be ready to move on to more complex recipes.

Keep it clean. Thoroughly clean your Instant Pot after each use. Unplug the unit. Remove and wash the silicone gasket, lid, and inner pot with hot, soapy water, rinse well, and air-dry completely before reassembly. Clean the inside rim of the outer pot with a small, damp brush and damp towel so food does not accumulate. (Never put water inside the outer pot.) Wash and dry the small cup on the outside of the unit, which catches drips and condensation.

OPERATIONS

The front panel of the Instant Pot is where you'll find cooking program and function keys, Warm and Cancel buttons, and an indicator panel that shows the pressure level and heat level and includes a timer. The panel will vary slightly according to your model, so consult your manual for complete directions on how to use and adjust the functions. The recipes in this book were tested on a 6-quart IP Duo Plus 60, IP Duo 60, and IP Ultra 60 but will work with any Instant Pot model.

Using the Instant Pot preprogrammed keys will always deliver excellent results. Nothing could be simpler than pressing the button that corresponds with the food you are cooking: Soup, Rice, Meat/Stew, and so on. Within most programs, you can adjust both time and pressure. But because I am a chef, I found myself sometimes using the Instant Pot more like a minikitchen and adjusting both times and function choices to achieve a particular result. As you grow confident, you may want to experiment.

The following are the cooking program keys used most in this book. For directions on using these and other keys, consult your manual. If you can't adjust a time in a preset cooking function on your model, switch to the Pressure Cook setting and adjust the time.

Cancel. Press the Cancel button to switch between different cooking functions (for example from Sauté to Soup) and press the Cancel button at the end of all cooking cycles. It is also your reset button if you need to stop cooking for any reason or change the timing of a dish. (Most models have a multipurpose button marked Keep Warm/Cancel; see facing page for how to use the Keep Warm function.)

Sauté. Many of the recipes in this book start with an initial sauté or browning step done right in the Instant Pot. Adjust the heat level between low, normal, and high as needed to prevent burning or to increase heat for a better sear. As you'll see in the recipes that follow, I only use Sauté—high when cooking beans, meat, or rice and when reducing sauces. Otherwise, I always use the Sauté—normal/medium setting. Check your manual for directions on how to adjust your model.

Simmer. There is no simmer key on the Instant Pot, but if you want to cook something just a little longer (which I often do with beans or soups), you can easily do this on the Sauté—low function.

Manual/Pressure Cook. Depending on your Instant Pot model, you may have a manual or pressure cook setting; both function the same. I refer to this setting as Pressure Cook in my recipes. You can adjust the cooking time with this setting by using the + and – buttons. All recipes in this book are cooked on the function default setting, or High Pressure, unless otherwise noted.

Keep Warm. I use the Keep Warm function to hold food for serving, which makes it great for potlucks or parties. I never allow the cooker to go automatically to this function because I prefer to check (and taste) the finished dish for doneness first and then switch to it.

Quick Release vs. Natural Release. When a cooking cycle is complete, the recipe will indicate whether to release pressure through Quick Release or Natural Release. The type of food being cooked determines the type of release used. Quick Release drops the temperature in the Instant Pot to stop the cooking process so food does not overcook. Natural Release allows food to cool slowly in its own juices.

Quick Release. When the cooking cycle is complete, press **Cancel**. Keeping your face and hands well away from the lid, use a pair of tongs or the end of a long spoon to turn the steam release handle to Venting. A loud hiss of steam will come from the top of the cooker. The steam will stop after a few seconds and the pressure valve will drop, indicating that all pressure has been released. Then you can remove the lid. Remember that the food inside will still be very hot.

Natural Release. When the cooking cycle is complete, press Cancel. Set a timer for the noted cooling time, usually 20 to 30 minutes, and then open the steam release handle as directed above to release any remaining pressure. Wait for the pressure valve to drop and then remove the lid. The food inside will still be hot.

TIMING

Cooking times may vary according to the ingredients you use and can be adjusted according to your definition of done (see Cooking Charts on page 176). I like meat that stays in intact pieces but can easily be shredded. You may like your meat cooked until falling apart. With the Instant Pot, you have the ability to regulate pressure and time, often within a cooking function, so you can customize to your cooking preference.

If you're in a hurry, press Sauté—high, which will bring the Instant Pot to pressure faster by first bringing the contents to a boil. Then press Cancel, secure the lid, and choose the desired function.

Another way to get dinner on the table quickly is to use the stove top for browning or reducing when your Instant Pot is already being used. If both my Instant Pots are busy (which happens quite a lot), I might roast tomatoes, tomatillos, and chiles for my salsa in a foil-lined skillet to get a jump on the next step.

Pot Thoughts: Deb's Hacks and Tips

It's called the Instant Pot, not the *Magic* Pot. You get out of it what you put into it. Quality food always takes good ingredients and attention. The Instant Pot makes great food faster and easier, and who doesn't love that?

Most recipes can be made from start to finish in the Instant Pot, especially if you have two inner pots. Some recipes might call for the use of a skillet (see Timing, page 3) or broiler, but this is almost always optional.

Read the recipe all the way through. Before you start cooking, check to make sure you have all the ingredients prepped. Follow recipe directions carefully.

Great ingredients = great food. Always use the best, most flavorful, and freshest ingredients. *Everything* you put in the pot, including the cooking liquid, needs to be flavorful.

Preseason meats. Sprinkle lightly with salt and refrigerate for a few hours or overnight before cooking. This step improves the finished flavor.

Presoak beans. Presoaked beans will always come out soft and creamy and cook more quickly. Of course, you can cook beans without soaking, if you wish.

Use no more liquid than necessary. Flavors become diluted with too much liquid. Except when making soups, use as little liquid as possible to cook, which will intensify the flavor of your dish. Bear in mind that some ingredients (like tomatoes and chicken) will add natural moisture as they cook, and you can always add a dash more broth to a finished dish if you need to.

Build flavor right in the inner pot. Professional cooks create flavor by utilizing every bit of crust in the pan after browning meat, as well as the pan juices. Many of the recipes in this book begin right in the inner pot, with browning meat for soups and stews, or with cooking a flavorful sauce base using the Sauté function and building from there.

Small amounts of fat add flavor. Save that skimmed chicken, pork, and duck fat to use instead of vegetable oil for the initial sauté step in recipes for soups and braises.

Brown on aluminum foil. Skin-on poultry (chicken, duck, turkey) tends to stick and tear during browning. I have had success lining the bottom of the inner pot with foil and browning on that. Or you can brown after cooking (see below). This also works for roasting tomatoes and tomatillos.

Brown at the end, not the beginning. Try browning poultry after cooking to avoid tearing the skin. When the cooking cycle is complete, let the meat rest in the liquid for 15 minutes to absorb the juices. Remove from the pot, pat dry, and brown in a skillet or under a hot broiler just before serving. Other delicate items, such as meatballs, may also be browned after cooking.

Tuck under foil to keep in moisture. Placing a piece of foil over food creates a steam trap, which keeps in moisture. I recommend this if you are cooking white-meat chicken, or substituting chicken for beef or pork in any recipe. I wrap turkey completely in foil before cooking and use the technique for some desserts, too.

Use the long-handled wire rack. When steaming a recipe, I prefer to use the long-handled wire rack that comes with most Instant Pots. This makes it easy to insert and remove baking dishes and large foods from the Instant Pot. Always use heat-resistant gloves when removing the rack from a hot pot.

Steps build flavor. Multiple steps (such as toasting, soaking, pureeing, and frying dried chiles for a salsa) are typical of Mexican recipes, and build traditional flavor with every step. Don't skip them!

Less is more. Intensify the flavor of cooking juices and sauces by simmering them down right in the inner pot. Cooking juices can be thickened to make a pan sauce by adding a little cornstarch (mixed with a liquid) during the last couple of minutes of simmering.

Let food rest after cooking. Don't serve as soon as the timer goes off. It might be the pressure aspect of the Instant Pot, but I found that the flavor of everything I made improved when the food was allowed to rest—or, perhaps, decompress—for a short time before serving, at least 15 minutes and preferably 30 minutes to 1 hour. Seasoning corrected itself, spice flavors reappeared, and meats were more succulent. Braises, soups, and stews will taste even better the next day!

Use less salt. Season lightly in the beginning and correct the salt, if necessary, after cooking and a 15-minute rest.

Some like it hot, maybe. The heat from chiles tends to permeate the dish and intensify as the food cooks. Aim for medium heat, and if you like spicier food, have a bottle of hot sauce on the table.

Adjust cooking times. After making a recipe once, feel free to adjust the cooking time up or down.

Use Warm function judiciously. Once you have ended the cooking cycle and released the pressure, check the food for doneness and taste. Afterward, use the Warm function to keep food hot or to serve from the Instant Pot for a buffet.

Finish with freshness. Mexican food is always finished with a little fresh garnish just before it is served: a fresh salsa, diced onions, and chopped cilantro are common touches. Tacos perk up with a grating of salty cotija cheese, while stews and soups might benefit from a dollop of cooling creaminess in the form of Mexican crema.

Season *al gusto*. After the food is cooked to your liking and has rested for at least 15 minutes, be sure to give it one last taste before serving. Does it need a pinch of salt? A squeeze of lime? Make it taste great—*al gusto*!

Essential Kitchen Tools

Blender. A powerful blender with at least two speeds is a necessity for chile sauces and moles.

Comal or cast-iron skillet. A cast-iron griddle, or *comal*, or a cast-iron skillet is used to heat tortillas for tacos or burritos, to toast tortillas for tacos *dorado* (see page 110), or to char tomatoes or toast chiles (see Timing, page 3).

Food processor. A food processor with a 2-quart bowl, a single speed, and a pulse button is all you need.

Immersion blender. Also called a stick or handheld blender, this handy tool allows you to finish many sauces and soups right in the Instant Pot.

Strainer or Food Mill. An 8-inch metal coarse-mesh strainer is ideal for straining broths and chile sauces, rinsing rice or other ingredients, and sifting flour. With a hand-powered food mill, which sits over a bowl, you can crank out velvety moles and salsas faster and more efficiently than if you forced them through a strainer.

Utensils. Silicone and wooden spatulas are preferable to metal tools, which can scratch the Instant Pot inner pot. You will also need a large slotted spoon and a ladle for removing food from the inner pot and metal tongs for turning tortillas, chiles, or meat and for transferring hot foods.

Guide to Mexican Chiles

Mexican cooks make full use of the wide variety of chiles available to them, many of which are regional. The most widely used chiles are available in both fresh and dried forms, which are used in different ways. Chiles are primarily used to add flavor—not heat—and many famous dishes, such as mole, are not at all extra spicy.

Any recipe step involving fresh or dried chiles, such as roasting, toasting, soaking, pureeing, or frying them, is essential for developing authentic Mexican flavor and should never be skipped. If you're concerned a chile will be too spicy, remove the seeds and ribs or substitute a milder chile.

FRESH CHILES

Here are the fresh chiles most commonly used in Mexican cooking, listed from mildest to hottest.

Bell Peppers. Usually red or green, but also available in yellow, orange, or purple. They are reliably mild and may be substituted for any spicier chile.

Anaheim. Large and narrow, these pale green chiles are mild but have a true chile taste and can be substituted for spicier poblano chiles in any recipe. They must be roasted, peeled, and seeded (see How to Roast Fresh Chiles, right) before use. Dried Anaheims are also called California chiles.

Poblano. These large, shiny, dark green chiles have a rich, almost smoky flavor, but can also be spicy. I usually use a combination of poblano and Anaheim to get the best flavor and control the spice level. Like Anaheims, poblanos must be roasted, peeled, and seeded before use. When dried, they are called ancho or pasilla chiles.

New Mexico green. Similar in shape to Anaheim chiles, these are darker and predictably spicy—sometimes *very* spicy. They must be roasted, peeled, and seeded before use. Fresh New Mexico chiles are seasonal and are sometimes sold as Hatch chiles.

HOW TO ROAST FRESH CHILES

Fresh chiles are almost always roasted or charred to enhance their flavor before using them in a recipe. To roast larger chiles, such as poblanos, Anaheims, or New Mexico chiles, turn on a gas burner, set the whole chile directly in the flame, and turn occasionally with tongs until evenly blistered and lightly charred on all sides. Alternatively, char the chiles beneath a hot broiler, as close as possible to the heat element, turning as needed, until blistered and lightly blackened in spots. Wrap in paper towels until cool, then remove the stem, split open, and remove the seeds. Rub off the charred skin with a paper towel and proceed with the recipe as directed. To roast smaller fresh chiles, such as serranos or jalapeños, line the bottom of the Instant Pot with aluminum foil and press **Sauté**. (A heavy skillet over high heat may be used instead.) Place the whole chiles on the foil (without oil) and roast on all sides, turning occasionally, until blistered.

Jalapeño. Small, plump, and shiny green, sometimes with red patches, jalapeños always have a kick, but their level of intensity varies. Jalapeños may be minced (with or without their seeds) and added raw to fresh salsas, such as Pico de Gallo (page 139). Roasted and seeded, they may be used in salsas or cut into *rajas* (strips). Pickled jalapeños (page 149) are a favorite table condiment in Mexico. When ripe, dried, and smoked, they are known as chipotle or *chile meco*.

Serrano. Small, dark green, and slender, you can count on serranos to be spicy and to be hotter than jalapeños, with a bright flavor. They are usually used raw, sliced or minced (with or without their seeds). If jalapeños aren't quite hot enough for you, substitute serranos.

Habanero. If you want hot, this is your chile. This small, bright orange chile always has a pervasive burning heat that makes the lips tingle. Handle with caution, and wash your hands well after handling.

DRIED CHILES

The flavor of dried chiles is developed by toasting over direct heat, and blossoms into its full complexity when the chiles are soaked in a little water. Once soft, the chiles can be pureed and worked into the recipe by simmering them with other ingredients or frying them to intensify their flavor. (See Why Fry a Salsa, page 140.)

Toast chiles by putting them in a hot, dry pan or directly in the Instant Pot inner pot on Sauté. Press down firmly with a spatula until the chiles blister, soften, and darken, being careful not to burn them. Turn the chiles and repeat. Transfer the chiles to a bowl and pour boiling water over them as directed in the recipe. Once they have soaked for the time indicated, transfer the soaked chiles to a blender and puree with other ingredients according to the recipe instructions. Be sure to puree the chiles for several minutes, until perfectly smooth, scraping down the sides of the blender once or twice. At this point, you can pass the pureed chiles through a food mill or coarse-mesh strainer to remove any traces of skin or fiber from the sauce. The chile puree may now be used as directed in the recipe.

When purchasing dried chiles, make sure the chiles are flexible and not crumbly or dusty.

When handling dried chiles, wear gloves, if possible. Wipe each chile with a paper towel. Remove the stem, cut a slit down one side, remove all the seeds and ribs, and prepare as directed in the recipe.

The following are the dried chiles most commonly used in Mexican cooking, listed from mildest to hottest. Heat level of chiles may vary from chile to chile, and may be affected by where and in what season the chile was grown. Always check heat level and adjust the balance of chiles accordingly.

Ancho. Deep flavors of fruit, hay, tobacco, and chocolate characterize this wide, 3- to 4-inch-long, reddish black to black chile. Also known as pasilla, it is the dried form of the fresh poblano chile.

California. The dried form of the Anaheim chile, the California is narrow, deep red, and 4 to 6 inches long. It has a mild taste and a light fruity flavor and looks similar to the spicier guajillo chile. I usually recommend a combination of guajillo and California to control the heat level.

Guajillo. Guajillos are narrow, 4 to 6 inches long, and have smooth reddish to dark red skin. The most important chile in enchilada sauce, the guajillo has a pure chile flavor with more heat and better flavor than the California.

New Mexico. Similar in appearance to the guajillo, this chile may be dark red to reddish brown. It has a flavor similar to that of the ancho, but it will always be spicy—and sometimes very spicy.

Chipotle. Smoke-dried ripe jalapeño chiles, chipotles are light to medium brown with dry-looking, leathery skin. The flavor is smoky, slightly bitter, and very spicy. (Canned chipotle chiles in adobo are dried jalapeños cooked in a vinegar, garlic, and tomato sauce.)

Chile de árbol. A small, slender red chile with many seeds, this one is hot, with a bitter edge. Seeds may be removed or, for a hotter salsa, left in.

Mexican Ingredients

Top-quality, fresh ingredients guarantee good results, no matter what you make.

Achiote. A spice paste made from annatto seeds and other spices, achiote is sold in 4-ounce bars at Mexican and Caribbean markets. When cooked, the bright red paste imparts a unique, subtle flavor to recipes like Cochinita Pibil (page 79) and Achiote Chicken Tacos (page 39.) Wrapped and refrigerated, it lasts almost indefinitely. There is no substitute.

Agave syrup. Made from the juice of the agave plant, agave syrup has a neutral flavor. Use it to temper the heat of chiles (see Pork Belly with Agave-Chipotle Glaze, page 80).

Avocado. The best-tasting variety is the Hass avocado, which has dark, pebbly skin and pale green, creamy flesh with a high fat content. A ripe avocado should just yield to gentle pressure at the stem end.

Banana leaf. Also called *platano* or plantain leaves, banana leaves add a unique flavor when used to wrap tamales (pages 94 to 97) or Cochinita Pibil (page 79). They are best fresh, but frozen banana leaves can be used in a pinch. Look for them at well-stocked Latin or Asian grocers. Directions for preparing them are on page 97.

Beef. Well-marbled cuts of beef give the best results and flavor. Most of the recipes in this book use boneless beef chuck (sometimes packaged as "pot roast"). Always buy choice grade beef. Bargain (ungraded) beef has little taste, and prime beef will cost you more without any improvement in flavor. Avoid precut stew beef, which may contain odd bits and gristle. Do not trim off fat before cooking. It will add great flavor as it renders and can be removed at the end.

Broth. A richly flavorful broth elevates everything you make, from soups to *guisados* (thick stews), and adds nutritional value. Uno-Dos-Tres Shredded Chicken and Broth (page 154) and its beef counterpart (page 156) yield great-tasting broths and are quick and easy to make in the Instant Pot. I use the meat for other recipes and freeze the broth in 1-quart freezer bags, so I always have some on hand. In any recipe, you may substitute good-quality low-sodium or unsalted canned chicken or beef broth, diluted with an equal quantity of water.

Cheese. Monterey Jack cheese is mild and melts well, making it a good all-purpose choice. Chihuahua cheese, also known as *menonita*, is a mild block cheese that melts at a low temperature and does not turn stringy. Substitute a mild Muenster or Oaxaca cheese, which are similar to mozzarella and will form long strings when melted. Salty, crumbly cotija (also known as *cotixa*) is sprinkled on beans, soups, and tacos as a finishing touch. If you can't find it, substitute a dry aged goat cheese or a salty ricotta salata.

Chicharrón. Deep-fried pork skin is crispy, melt-in-the-mouth bits of golden yumminess. Use small pieces to add crunch and flavor to dishes like Pork Albóndigas in Green Sauce with Chicharrón (page 76). It's also great on a taco or sprinkled on Nopales Salad (page 114.) Chicharrón will soften slightly in a salsa or salad.

Chicken. The better the chicken, the better the dish. Free-range chicken (preferably organic) is the best-tasting chicken around. As in Mexico, some recipes in this book call for cooking whole chicken pieces, complete with the skin and bones, which add flavor. It is easy to remove the skin and bones before serving. You can, however, substitute the same weight of boneless chicken. Be careful not to overcook chicken: it can easily turn into a paste. The chicken is done when you can easily slip the tip of a knife into the thickest part. Chicken must be cooked to an internal temperature of 165°F.

Chocolate. Mexican chocolate comes mixed with ground almonds, sugar, cinnamon, and cardamom. The best brand is Ibarra, which is sold in a distinctive red-and-yellow box. A tiny amount of chocolate is used in the Chicken Mole (page 34.) Try grating a little on ice cream or whipped cream.

Corn. Fresh corn is called *elote*. Grilled, boiled, or cooked on a griddle with butter and chiles (Corn Esquites, page 105), it is a favorite snack in Mexico.

Crema. Thick Mexican crema is a luscious garnish for soups, enchiladas, or desserts. Quality commercial sour cream may be substituted.

Fresh lard. A semiliquid rendered pork fat, fresh lard is sold in tubs at Mexican markets. You can also use the white fat that is rendered when making Carnitas (page 73). Fresh lard smells and tastes delicious—like carnitas—and it adds a subtle, rich flavor. If you don't have access to fresh lard or carnitas fat, use a neutral vegetable oil, such as corn or canola oil, or all-vegetable shortening instead. Do not substitute the blocks of white lard sold in supermarkets, which is a hydrogenated fat used in baking and making tortillas.

Garlic. For the best flavor, buy whole heads of fresh garlic and peel the cloves as needed. (Prepeeled or minced garlic, sold at some stores, tastes foul; your cooking deserves better!) To peel garlic, tap the clove with the side of a chef's knife to loosen the skin and remove it. When mincing garlic, slice it first and then sprinkle it with a pinch of salt before mincing. The salt will prevent the garlic from sticking to the knife.

Limes. Freshly cut limes are served alongside many soups and tacos. A bright spritz of lime juice wakes up the flavor of food in a way no other seasoning can. Key limes—small, thin-skinned, yellowish limes—have the best flavor. Do not substitute lemon juice or bottled lime juice.

Masa. Dough made from dried corn that has been treated with ground lime (*cal*) and boiled. Masa can be made as needed from masa harina (see Basic Tamales, page 94), purchased fresh from the *tortillerias* found in many Mexican markets, or made from scratch.

Nopales. Nopales are the small, tender paddles of the beavertail cactus. The thorns are scraped off and the paddles are cut up and boiled until tender. Their delicious flavor is similar to cooked green beans.

HERBS

Cilantro. Fresh cilantro has a distinctive smell and taste. It's a necessity in fresh salsas, is always used as a garnish on tacos, and plays a leading role in Salsa Verde (page 140) and Arroz Verde (page 131). The fresh taste disappears quickly, so chop it just before using it. There is no substitute for the flavor, but if you dislike cilantro, minced flat-leaf parsley can be used instead to add a touch of green to dishes.

Epazote. A native of the Americas, epazote has a strong and unusual flavor reminiscent of both oregano and mint. Generous handfuls flavor corn, beans, *guisados*, and soups. Dried epazote leaves may be substituted for fresh. I buy it fresh whenever I see it and dry it myself. Epazote is easy to grow in a kitchen garden in most climate zones. Fresh or dried marjoram in small quantities may be substituted.

Marjoram. This mildly flavored herb, which was introduced to Mexico by Spanish monks in the sixteenth century, tastes like an earthy, floral oregano.

Mexican oregano. Mexican oregano is very fragrant, with a sweeter and milder flavor than Mediterranean (Greek or Italian) oregano. It is available dried at Mexican markets. If you can't get Mexican oregano, substitute fresh or dried marjoram

Parsley. This mildly flavored, leafy herb can be sprinkled on dishes for a burst of green color and fresh flavor, added to soups, or stirred into a meat mixture to make *albóndigas* (meatballs). As noted above, if you can't abide cilantro, substitute parsley.

Nopales, which are nutrient rich, may be served as a salad (page 114) or added to any *guisado*. They can be purchased at Mexican and Latin produce markets.

Oil. For cooking, use a neutral-flavored vegetable oil, such as canola or corn oil. Use olive oil where specified.

Onions. Yellow onions should be used *only* for cooking. Raw white or red onions, mixed with cilantro, are a common table condiment and the perfect finish for a flavorful taco. For fresh salsas, such as Pico de Gallo (page 139), or a garnish, use white or red onions. Raw onions may be rinsed with cold water and drained to tone down their flavor.

Piloncillo. Dark brown, mildly sweet raw sugar, with a gentle molasses taste, *piloncillo* is sold in rock-hard cones that must be crushed before use. It is generally dissolved in liquid, but it is also delicious sprinkled on cakes or fruit. To crush, place the sugar in a plastic bag, wrap in a kitchen towel, and pound with a mallet or a small skillet. Dark brown cane sugar is a good substitute.

Plantains. Known in Mexico as *plátano machos*, plantains are large, starchy members of the banana family. Plantains are sold at Asian, Mexican, Latin, and Caribbean markets. Choose plantains that are firm, have yellow skin, and are still green at the tip. Avoid those with skin that has turned black.

Pork. Boneless pork shoulder (also known as pork butt) is the perfect choice for many recipes in this book, from carnitas to *guisados*. Do not trim the fat before cooking; it will add terrific flavor as it renders and can be removed after cooking.

Potatoes. Choose firm White Rose, red, or Yukon gold potatoes if you want them to stay in whole pieces. For mashing, russet or Yukon gold are best.

Rice. Most Instant Pot recipes work best with long-grain white or brown rice. Short-grain Arborio rice is the best choice for rice puddings. Do not use Asian short-grain rice. For cooking tips, see Arroz Perfecto (page 130).

Salt. Use kosher or sea salt; iodized table salt has a slight bitterness.

Sausage, chorizo. Mexican chorizo is a fresh, soft pork or beef sausage flavored with garlic, dried chiles, black pepper, and vinegar. It must be thoroughly cooked before eating. Do not substitute Spanish or Filipino chorizos, which are dried sausages.

Spices. Because of Spanish influences on Mexican cuisine during colonization in the sixteenth century, Ceylon cinnamon, cloves, and other sweet spices appear in many savory dishes, such as moles, along with black pepper. Other common spices include native allspice (which tastes like a cross between pepper and cinnamon), bay leaf, and cumin.

Stock. See Broth.

Tomatillos. They resemble small green tomatoes in papery husks and taste fresh and acidic. Choose small to medium tomatillos for the best results. Before using, remove the husks and wash the tomatillos well with warm water to remove their sticky coating.

Tomatoes. Meaty Roma tomatoes are the best choice for Mexican cooking. Other types of tomatoes are too juicy and full of seeds. The flavor of fresh tomatoes can be intensified by charring or pureeing seeded tomatoes in a blender and frying the puree. To char tomatoes, line the bottom of the Instant Pot inner pot (or a heavy skillet) with aluminum foil and press Sauté. Place the whole tomatoes directly on the foil (don't add any oil) and allow them to blacken before turning them. Char on all sides. In cooked dishes, fire-roasted canned tomatoes in juice are an acceptable substitute.

Tortillas. Fresh, warm corn tortillas make an appearance at nearly every meal, and of course, you can't have an authentic taco without a corn tortilla. (See page 158 to make your own.)

chapter 1

SOUPS

CHICKEN-TORTILLA SOUP

Serves 2 to 4

2 guajillo chiles, stemmed, seeded, and torn into pieces

1 cup boiling water

2 Roma tomatoes

2 tomatillos, husked and roughly chopped

2 garlic cloves, peeled

½ large white onion, finely diced (about ¾ cup), plus ¼ cup diced white onion for serving

1 tablespoon vegetable oil

½ small carrot, peeled and cut into matchsticks or small dice

½ Anaheim chile, seeded and diced (about ¼ cup)

1½ pounds boneless, skinless chicken thighs

6 cups chicken broth

1 teaspoon kosher salt

2 cups toasted corn tortilla strips or tortilla chips, broken into bite-size pieces

½ cup shredded Monterey Jack or Cheddar cheese

1 ripe avocado, halved, pitted, peeled, and diced

¼ cup chopped fresh cilantro leaves

4 lime wedges

This classic recipe is Mexican home cooking at its best, and the perfect place to showcase a flavorful chicken broth. Serve in big bowls with lime wedges on the side. For advice on selecting and prepping tomatillos, see page 13.

Place the chile pieces in a blender and pour in the boiling water. Let soak for 10 minutes, until the chiles are softened, then drain off and discard the water.

Cut 1 tomato into quarters and scoop out and discard the core and seeds. Roughly chop the quarters and add to the blender. Core, seed, and finely dice the second tomato and set aside.

Add the tomatillos, garlic, and ½ cup of the finely diced onion and blend until very smooth, scraping down the blender as needed. Do not add any water.

Press **Sauté—high** on the Instant Pot and heat the oil. Add the diced tomato, the remaining finely diced onion, the carrot, and the Anaheim chile and sauté for about 1 minute, until beginning to soften. Add the chile puree and cook, stirring, until the mixture is quite dry and beginning to stick to the pot. Press **Cancel**. Add the chicken, broth, and salt. Secure the lid and set the Pressure Release to **Sealing**. Press **Soup**, then set the cooking time for 20 minutes.

When the cooking program is complete, press **Cancel**. Perform a quick pressure release by moving the Pressure Release to **Venting**. Open the pot, then transfer the chicken to a plate. Using two forks, shred the chicken into bite-size pieces. Divide the chicken evenly among heated bowls. Top each portion with the tortilla strips, cheese, and diced onion, then ladle the hot broth over the top. Garnish with the avocado and cilantro and serve right away, with the lime wedges.

BEEF AND CORN ALBÓNDIGAS SOUP

Albóndigas (meatballs) are fun to make and eat; here they're packed with the flavors of smoky bacon and warming cumin and chipotle. This satisfying soup is a terrific main course on a chilly night. Round out the meal with a side salad and white rice (page 134). The better the quality of the broth you use, the better the soup will turn out, so do use homemade beef broth. The garnish of chicharrón (deep-fried pork skin) adds a deliciously crunchy counterpoint to the tender meatballs.

In a blender, combine the tomatoes and 1 garlic clove, blend until smooth, then transfer to a bowl.

In a food processor, combine the onion and the remaining 4 garlic cloves and pulse until very finely chopped. Transfer to a different, large bowl. Add the diced bacon to the food processor and pulse until finely chopped. Add to the bowl of onions and garlic, along with the salt, black pepper, cumin, red pepper flakes, egg white, half of the cilantro, the corn, and ¾ cup of the cotija cheese. Stir until combined, then add the ground beef and, using your hands, mix thoroughly until all of the ingredients are evenly distributed. Shape the mixture with moistened hands into 24 balls, each 1½ to 2 inches in diameter, and place them on a plate as you go.

Press **Sauté—high** on the Instant Pot and heat the oil. Add the meatballs in a single layer, working in batches if necessary, and cook, turning occasionally, until lightly browned on all sides, about 5 minutes. Transfer to a clean plate. Add the pureed tomatoes to the pot and cook, stirring occasionally, until thickened, about 5 minutes, scraping up any browned bits on the bottom of the pot.

Serves 4 to 6

2 Roma tomatoes, cored

5 large garlic cloves, peeled

½ small white onion, roughly chopped

3 slices thick-cut bacon, diced

1 teaspoon kosher salt

1 teaspoon freshly ground black pepper

1 teaspoon ground cumin

½ teaspoon red pepper flakes

1 large egg white

⅓ cup minced fresh cilantro leaves

1 cup fresh, cooked or thawed frozen corn kernels

4 ounces cotija cheese, crumbled (1 cup)

1 pound ground beef (90% lean)

3 tablespoons vegetable oil

8 cups Uno-Dos-Tres beef broth (page 156)

FOR SERVING

Chipotle chile powder

Diced white onion

Crumbled chicharrón

Lime wedges

CONTINUED

Return the meatballs to the pot, then pour in the broth. Press **Cancel**. Secure the lid and set the Pressure Release to **Sealing**. Press **Pressure Cook**, then set the cooking time for 5 minutes.

When the cooking program is complete, press **Cancel**. Perform a quick pressure release by moving the Pressure Release to **Venting**. Open the pot, then stir in the remaining cilantro. Taste and adjust the seasoning with salt if needed.

Using a slotted spoon, divide the albóndigas evenly among warmed bowls. Ladle the hot broth over the top. Sprinkle each bowl with 1 tablespoon of the remaining cotija cheese and serve right away, passing the chipotle chile powder, diced onion, chicharrón, and lime wedges on the side.

VARIATIONS

For turkey and corn albóndigas, substitute ground dark-meat turkey for the beef. Or for chicken and corn albóndigas, use ground dark-meat chicken.

For a version with kale and/or potatoes, add 1 cup shredded kale leaves and/or 4 ounces Yukon gold potatoes, peeled and diced, after pouring in the broth.

PINTO BEAN SOUP WITH CHORIZO AND FRIED TORTILLAS

This soup is rich, flavorful, and indulgent—so much so that it almost seems over the top. But pinto beans, like all beans, are nutritious and healthful. Make the soup vegetarian by using soy chorizo and omitting the bacon and ham hock from the pinto beans. Once you've made the Cowboy Pinto Beans, the soup comes together in minutes.

In a small, heavy skillet, warm the oil over medium-high heat until shimmering. Add the tortilla squares and cook, stirring frequently, for 1 to 2 minutes, until golden brown and crisp. Using a slotted spoon, transfer the squares to a paper towel–lined plate to drain.

To the same skillet, add the chorizo. Cook over medium-high heat, breaking up the meat into small pieces with the back of a wooden spoon, 6 to 8 minutes, until cooked through.

Using an immersion blender, puree the beans (and the meat and chile pieces) directly in the Instant Pot until smooth. Taste and adjust the seasoning with salt and pepper if needed. Ladle the soup into warmed bowls and drizzle with the crema. Top with the chorizo and pico de gallo, then scatter with the fried tortilla squares. Sprinkle with onion (if using) and serve right away.

Serves 4

2 tablespoons vegetable oil

2 corn tortillas, cut into ½-inch squares

4 ounces Mexican-style chorizo sausage, casing removed

1 recipe Cowboy Pinto Beans (page 129), just cooked and still hot

Kosher salt and freshly ground black pepper

⅓ cup Mexican crema or sour cream

⅓ cup Pico de Gallo (page 139)

Diced white or red onion or thinly sliced green onions, green parts only, for serving (optional)

BLACK BEAN SOUP

Serves 4 to 6

1½ cups dried black beans

2 tablespoons vegetable oil

1 small white or yellow onion, diced (about 1 cup)

4 garlic cloves, minced

3 tablespoons soy bacon bits (optional)

1½ teaspoons ground cumin

1½ teaspoons smoked paprika or ancho chile powder

1½ teaspoons dried Mexican oregano

1 bay leaf

½ teaspoon freshly ground black pepper

1 guajillo chile, stemmed, seeded, and torn into pieces

1 teaspoon red pepper flakes, or 1 chile de árbol

2 teaspoons kosher salt

6 cups water or vegetable broth, plus more as needed

One 14½-ounce can diced fire-roasted tomatoes and their liquid, chopped

10 fresh epazote leaves, shredded

Black beans, also called turtle beans, have a rich, naturally smoky flavor. This soup is satisfying on its own for a light lunch or dinner or, in smaller servings, to round out a meal of tacos. With the Instant Pot, you can have it on the table in an hour. For a creamier texture, I recommend presoaking the beans overnight. Epazote is a native herb with a strong, peppery flavor and the scent of marjoram.

Place the beans in a large bowl, cover with 4 cups water, and let soak overnight at room temperature. Drain the beans.

Press **Sauté—normal/medium** on the Instant Pot and heat the oil. Add the onion, garlic, and soy bacon bits (if using) and cook, stirring occasionally, for about 2 minutes, until softened. Add the cumin, paprika, oregano, bay, black pepper, guajillo chile, and red pepper flakes. Cook, stirring, for 1 minute. Press **Cancel**.

Add the drained beans to the pot, along with the salt, water, tomatoes with their liquid, and the epazote. Secure the lid and set the Pressure Release to **Sealing**. Press **Beans**, then set the cooking time for 30 minutes.

When the cooking program is complete, press **Cancel**. Allow the pressure to release naturally for 30 minutes, then move the Pressure Release to **Venting** to release any remaining steam. Open the pot and taste a bean—it should be creamy and tender. If it is not, secure the lid once again and set the Pressure Release to **Sealing**. Press **Pressure Cook**, then set the cooking time for 5 minutes.

When the cooking program is complete, press **Cancel**. Let the pressure release naturally for 10 minutes, then move the Pressure Release to **Venting** to release any remaining steam.

Remove and discard the bay leaf. Place an immersion blender in the pot and pulse a couple of times, which will thicken the soup slightly without pureeing. Taste and adjust the seasoning with salt and pepper if needed. Ladle the soup into warmed bowls and garnish with sour cream, cilantro, green onions, and pico de gallo. Serve right away, passing the hot sauce on the side.

NOTES For added richness, top the soup with grated cotija cheese; cooked and crumbled Mexican-style chorizo sausage; shredded, cooked chicken or beef; diced ham; or crumbled cooked bacon.

To make Basic Black Beans (for serving as a side dish or as a filling for burritos and tamales), do not puree the beans. Taste and adjust the seasoning with salt and pepper to taste.

FOR SERVING

Sour cream or plain
Greek yogurt

Chopped fresh cilantro leaves

Sliced green onions, green
parts only

Pico de Gallo (page 139)

Habanero hot sauce
(page 144)

CHICKEN AND LENTIL SOUP WITH GREENS

Serves 4 to 6

2 tablespoons vegetable oil

8 ounces boneless, skinless chicken thighs or breasts, cut into 1-inch pieces

½ white or yellow onion, diced

1 celery stalk, diced

1 carrot, peeled and diced

4 garlic cloves, minced

2 bay leaves

1 teaspoon fresh thyme leaves or marjoram leaves, or ½ teaspoon dried thyme or marjoram

¼ teaspoon minced fresh rosemary leaves

1 teaspoon kosher salt

½ teaspoon freshly ground black pepper

2 cups green or brown lentils, rinsed and drained

3 cups chicken broth

3 cups water

4 cups arugula; stemmed and shredded kale; stemmed and shredded chard; or trimmed and shredded ramps

Garden greens and wild greens, such as chard and purslane, play a big role in traditional Mexican cooking. Here they add great flavor and bump up the nutritional value of this simple soup, which cooks up in about 30 minutes. For a different flavor, replace the chicken with smoked chicken or turkey.

Press **Sauté—normal/medium** on the Instant Pot and heat the oil. Add the chicken and cook, stirring occasionally, for about 5 minutes, until lightly browned. Add the onion, celery, carrot, and garlic and cook, stirring occasionally, for about 5 minutes, until the vegetables have softened. Add the bay, thyme, and rosemary, then press **Cancel**. Stir in the salt, pepper, lentils, broth, and water.

Secure the lid and set the Pressure Release to **Sealing**. Press **Soup**, then set the cooking time for 20 minutes.

When the cooking program is complete, press **Cancel**. Perform a quick pressure release by moving the Pressure Release to **Venting**. Open the pot, then stir in the greens. Replace the lid without securing it and let stand for 15 minutes, until the greens wilt. Taste and adjust the seasoning with salt and pepper if needed. Ladle the soup into warmed bowls and serve right away.

VARIATIONS

For a smoky version, use 8 ounces smoked (cooked) chicken or turkey, cut into 1-inch pieces, instead of boneless, skinless chicken. (You can buy smoked chicken or turkey thighs at most grocery stores.)

For a version with "wild" greens, use sliced ramps, stemmed lamb's-quarters, or purslane in place of the arugula, kale, or chard.

For a version with sprouted lentils, substitute an equal amount of sprouted lentils for the green or brown lentils.

CHICKEN ENCHILADA SOUP

I always keep chicken broth and salsa in my freezer, frozen flat in freezer-safe plastic bags. These useful items can be quickly turned into a meal, like this yummy soup, which contains all the flavor of chicken enchiladas without the fuss. And with the Instant Pot, it's on the table in about 20 minutes. Taste for seasoning at the end of cooking, since both the broth and Red Chile Salsa contain salt.

Press **Sauté—high** on the Instant Pot and heat the oil. Add the chicken, onion, and garlic and cook, stirring occasionally, for about 5 minutes, until the chicken is opaque and onion is softened. Add the rice, zucchini, and salt and cook, stirring occasionally, for 2 minutes, until the rice is translucent. Stir in the broth and red chile salsa, then press **Cancel**.

Secure the lid and set the Pressure Release to **Sealing**. Press **Soup**, then set the cooking time for 20 minutes.

When the cooking program is complete, press **Cancel**. Perform a quick pressure release by moving the Pressure Release to **Venting**.

Open the pot, then taste and adjust the seasoning with salt if needed. Ladle the soup into warmed bowls and top with a spoonful of sour cream and a sprinkle of green onions.

VARIATIONS

For Chicken Enchilada Soup with Corn, add 1 cup fresh or thawed frozen corn kernels along with the zucchini.

Serves 4 to 6

2 tablespoons vegetable oil

1½ pounds boneless, skinless chicken thighs, cut into ½-inch pieces

1 small white or yellow onion, diced (about 1 cup)

2 large garlic cloves, minced

½ cup long-grain white rice, rinsed and drained

1 small zucchini, diced

1 teaspoon kosher salt

4 cups chicken broth

4 cups Red Chile Salsa (page 141) or store-bought red enchilada sauce

Sour cream for serving

Thinly sliced green onions, green parts only, or diced white onion for serving

RED POSOLE WITH PORK

Serves 4 to 6

1 teaspoon plus 1 tablespoon vegetable oil

2 guajillo chiles, stemmed, seeded, and torn into pieces

2 California or ancho chiles, stemmed, seeded, and torn into pieces

1 chile de árbol, stemmed and seeded

¾ cup boiling water

½ small white or yellow onion, diced

4 large garlic cloves, sliced

2 teaspoons ground cumin

2 teaspoons oregano

1 tablespoon kosher salt

½ teaspoon black peppercorns

5½ cups beef or chicken broth or water

1 pound meaty pork bones

1 pound beef shank bones or meaty oxtails

1 smoked pork hock (about 12 ounces)

1½ pounds boneless pork shoulder, cut into 4 pieces

One 28-ounce can white hominy with liquid

Posole is not just a soup, it's an event: a big hearty bowl of goodness, sumptuous and filling, and totally worth the effort of a couple of extra steps. The bones are essential; use bigger ones so they are easier to handle at the end. I like to cook a bone-in pork shoulder for this and use the big blade bone. The pork hock adds subtle smoky notes, while the beef bones or oxtails add to the soup's complexity. Frying the chile puree improves the flavor of the soup, so don't skip this step.

———————

Press **Sauté—normal/medium** on the Instant Pot and heat the 1 teaspoon oil. Add the guajillo, California, and árbol chiles and cook, stirring occasionally, for about 3 minutes, until fragrant. Press **Cancel**.

Transfer the chiles to a blender and pour in the boiling water. Let soak for 10 minutes, until the chiles have softened, then pour off and discard the water.

Add onion, garlic, cumin, oregano, salt, peppercorns, and ½ cup of the broth to the blender. Puree until very smooth, scraping down the blender as needed.

Press **Sauté—normal/medium** on the Instant Pot and heat the remaining 1 tablespoon oil. Add the chile puree and cook, stirring occasionally, for about 5 minutes, until thickened and slightly darkened; be careful not to burn the puree. Press **Cancel**.

Place the pork and beef bones and the pork hock in the pot. Arrange the pork shoulder pieces evenly on top. Pour the hominy and its liquid over the meat, then pour in the remaining 5 cups broth.

Secure the lid and set the Pressure Release to **Sealing**. Press **Meat/Stew**, then set the cooking time for 30 minutes.

CONTINUED

FOR SERVING

Finely shredded green cabbage

Hot sauce or red pepper flakes

Lime wedges

Diced white onion

Chopped fresh cilantro leaves

Warmed tortillas

Dried Mexican oregano (optional)

Sliced radishes (optional)

When the cooking program is complete, perform a quick pressure release by moving the Pressure Release handle to **Venting**. Press the **Keep Warm** setting.

Open the pot. Using tongs, transfer the bones and the pork hock to a plate; leave the pork shoulder in the pot. When cool enough to handle, remove any meat from the bones and hock, shredding it into bite-size pieces. Add the meat back to the pot; discard the skin and bones.

Using a spoon, skim off and discard as much fat as possible from the surface of the posole. Using the tongs, transfer the pieces of pork shoulder to a cutting board, chop them into 1-inch pieces, and return to the pot. Taste and adjust the seasoning with salt and pepper if needed. Ladle the posole into warmed bowls and serve right away with the cabbage, hot sauce, lime wedges, onion, cilantro, warmed tortillas, oregano (if using), and radishes (if using) on the side.

NOTE To make the posole as fat-free as possible, prepare it in advance, transfer to an airtight container, and refrigerate it for up to 2 days. Before reheating, use a spoon to remove the congealed layer of fat from the surface.

VARIATION

For Red Posole with Chicken, substitute 1½ pounds boneless, skinless chicken thighs for the pork shoulder and reduce the cooking time to 20 minutes. After the pressure has released, using tongs, transfer the chicken to a cutting board, shred with two forks, and return the shredded chicken to the soup.

POTATO AND CHEESE SOUP WITH CHIPOTLE

This rustic soup is usually made with Chihuahua cheese (see page 9), which melts with the heat of the broth. Monterey Jack or a mild Gouda is a good substitute. If you want a spicier soup, add an extra tablespoon of the adobo sauce from the chipotles at the end.

Press **Sauté—normal/medium** on the Instant Pot and heat the butter until melted. Add the onion and garlic and cook, stirring occasionally, for about 2 minutes, until they start to soften. Add the tomatoes and Anaheim chiles and cook, stirring occasionally, for about 2 minutes more, until just starting to soften. Stir in the potatoes, broth, chipotle chile, salt, and oregano. Press **Cancel**.

Secure the lid and set the Pressure Release to **Sealing**. Press **Soup**, then set the cooking time for 20 minutes.

When the cooking program is complete, press **Cancel**. Perform a quick pressure release by moving the Pressure Release to **Venting**.

Open the pot, then press **Sauté—normal/medium** and bring the soup to a boil. In a small bowl, stir together the cornstarch and milk, then whisk the mixture into the soup. Bring to a simmer, stirring constantly, and cook for about 2 minutes, until thickened.

Press **Cancel**, then stir in the cilantro. Add the Chihuahua cheese and stir until the cheese has melted and the soup is smooth. Taste and adjust the seasoning with salt if needed. Ladle the soup into warmed bowls and sprinkle with the cotija cheese and green onions. Serve right away.

VARIATION
For a vegetarian version, substitute vegetable broth for the chicken broth.

Serves 4

2 tablespoons butter

1 small white or yellow onion, diced

3 large garlic cloves, minced

2 Roma tomatoes, cored, seeded, and finely diced

2 Anaheim chiles, stemmed, seeded, and finely diced

1 pound red or Yukon gold potatoes, peeled and cut into ½-inch chunks

5 cups chicken broth

1½ tablespoons chopped chipotle chile in adobo sauce

1 tablespoon kosher salt

½ teaspoon dried Mexican oregano

¼ cup cornstarch

1 cup whole milk

Leaves from ¼ bunch cilantro, chopped

2½ cups shredded Chihuahua cheese, Monterey Jack cheese, or Gouda cheese (8 ounces)

2 tablespoons grated cotija cheese

Thinly sliced green onions, green parts only, for serving

CREAMY MUSHROOM SOUP WITH EPAZOTE

Serves 4

¼ cup dried porcini mushrooms

8 dried shiitake mushrooms, stemmed

2 cups boiling water

1 small white or yellow onion, roughly chopped

2 large garlic cloves

½ small celery stalk, roughly chopped

8 ounces cremini mushrooms, cut into quarters

8 ounces white mushrooms, cut into quarters

4 ounces fresh shiitake mushrooms, stemmed and cut into quarters

1 tablespoon olive oil

1½ tablespoons butter

6 cups chicken broth or vegetable broth

10 fresh epazote leaves, shredded, or ½ teaspoon dried marjoram

1 tablespoon kosher salt

¼ cup cornstarch

½ cup white wine

1 cup heavy cream or whole milk

2 teaspoons freshly ground black pepper

1 large poblano chile, roasted (see page 6), seeded, peeled, and cut into ¼-inch dice

Mushrooms, roasted poblano chile, and epazote are often used together in Mexican cooking. The strong flavor of epazote creates a unique counterpoint to the rich flavors of mushrooms and spicy chiles. This luxurious, umami-rich soup includes five types of mushrooms as well as wine and cream. Make it for dinner when you're not in a rush, or save it for a special occasion. Charring the poblano brings out its unique taste and adds a smoky note.

In a heatproof bowl, combine the porcini and dried shiitake mushrooms. Pour in the boiling water and let stand for about 5 minutes, until the mushrooms are softened.

In a food processor, combine the onion, garlic, and celery, then pulse until finely chopped. Transfer to a small bowl and set aside. Add the cremini, white, and fresh shiitake mushrooms to the food processor and pulse until chopped into ¼-inch pieces. Transfer to a separate bowl and set aside. Pour the soaked mushrooms and liquid into a wire-mesh strainer set over a bowl. Add the drained mushrooms to the food processor; reserve the soaking liquid. Pulse until the mushrooms are finely chopped.

Press **Sauté—normal/medium** on the Instant Pot and heat the oil and butter until the butter melts. Add the onion mixture and cook, stirring occasionally, for about 2 minutes, until the mushrooms start to soften. Add the soaked dried mushrooms and cook, stirring occasionally, for about 5 minutes, until they begin to stick to the pot. Add the fresh mushrooms and cook, stirring occasionally, for about 5 minutes, until the mushrooms start to soften and release their liquid. Stir in the reserved mushroom soaking liquid, broth, epazote, and salt. Press **Cancel**.

Secure the lid and set the Pressure Release to **Sealing**. Press **Pressure Cook**, then set the cooking time for 5 minutes.

When the cooking program is complete, press **Cancel**. Perform a quick pressure release by moving the Pressure Release to **Venting**.

Open the pot, then press **Sauté—normal/medium** and bring the soup to a boil. In a small bowl, stir together the cornstarch and wine, then whisk the mixture into the soup. Bring to a simmer, stirring constantly, and cook for about 2 minutes, until thickened. Stir in the cream, pepper, and poblano chile, then cook for about 5 minutes.

Press **Cancel**, then taste and adjust the seasoning with salt and pepper if needed. Lade the soup into warmed bowls and serve right away.

chapter 2

POULTRY

CHICKEN MOLE

Serves 4 to 6

1 tablespoon vegetable oil

4 pounds bone-in, skin-on chicken thighs (about 10 thighs)

1½ teaspoons kosher salt

MOLE

3 large pasilla or ancho chiles, stemmed, seeded, and torn into pieces

3 California or guajillo chiles, stemmed, seeded, and torn into pieces

One 6-inch corn tortilla, torn into pieces

¼ cup skin-on peanuts

¼ cup blanched almonds

2 tablespoons white sesame seeds

¼ cup diced white or yellow onion

1 garlic clove, sliced

1 Roma tomato, cored and cut into eighths

½ firm banana, peeled and sliced

¼ teaspoon dried Mexican oregano

1 whole clove

One 1-inch piece cinnamon stick, or ½ teaspoon ground cinnamon

10 black peppercorns

This Instant Pot mole is simple and quick and tastes every bit as good as a traditional mole, which takes all day. Read the recipe through and follow the steps in order, as you are building the flavor right in the inner pot. The last steps of frying and straining the mole boost its flavor and make it smooth and sweet. I suggest using bone-in chicken thighs because the meat stays firm and juicy, and the thighs are easier to serve. This mole is even better the next day.

Press **Sauté—high** on the Instant Pot and heat the oil. Working in batches, add the chicken in a single layer and cook until well browned on both sides, about 4 minutes per side. Transfer to a large plate. After all the chicken has been browned, season with salt and set aside.

To make the mole: Add chile and tortilla pieces to the pot and cook, stirring, for about 1 minute. Add the peanuts, almonds, and sesame seeds and cook, stirring occasionally, for about 2 minutes, until the peanuts and seeds are lightly golden, scraping up any browned bits on the bottom of the pot. Stir in the onion, garlic, tomato, banana, oregano, clove, cinnamon, and peppercorns. Cook, stirring, for about 1 minute. Press **Cancel**. Pour in the broth and scrape up any browned bits from the bottom of the pot. Return the chicken thighs to the pot, arranging them in an even layer, then pour in any accumulated juices.

Secure the lid and set the Pressure Release to **Sealing**. Press **Meat/Stew**, then set the cooking time for 20 minutes.

When the cooking program is complete, press **Cancel**. Perform a quick pressure release by moving the Pressure Release to **Venting**. Uncover the pot and let cool for 20 minutes. Using tongs, transfer the chicken to a large plate and cover with aluminum foil to keep warm.

Working in batches, transfer the contents of the Instant Pot to a blender and puree until very smooth. Pour each batch into a bowl before pureeing the next.

Heat a large skillet over medium heat for about 3 minutes, then pour in the puree. Cover with a splatter guard (optional) and cook, stirring occasionally, for about 20 minutes, until the puree has thickened and darkened in color. Add the chocolate and stir until melted.

Process the mole through a food mill, or set a coarse wire-mesh strainer over a bowl and scrape in the mole. Using a rubber spatula, force it through the strainer to remove chile skins and other gritty bits. Discard the solids in the strainer, then return the mole to the skillet.

Set the skillet over medium heat and cook, stirring, for about 3 minutes, until the mole is hot. Taste and season with salt and sugar, adding the sugar about ¼ teaspoon at a time until the flavors are balanced. (Add only enough sugar to enhance the flavors; the mole should not taste sweet.) Add the chicken and any accumulated juices and make sure the chicken is nestled into the sauce, then cook for about 5 minutes, just until heated through. Serve the mole sprinkled with sesame seeds and a few onion rings and with rice, warmed tortillas, and beans on the side.

4 cups chicken broth

2 tablespoons roughly chopped Mexican chocolate, preferably Ibarra (see page 10), or 2 tablespoons dark chocolate chips

Kosher salt

Up to 1 tablespoon sugar

FOR SERVING

White sesame seeds

Thin red onion rings

Arroz Blanco (page 134)

Warmed corn tortillas

Cowboy Pinto Beans (page 129)

GARLIC-CHILE CHICKEN

Serves 4

1½ pounds bone-in, skin-on chicken thighs (about 4 thighs)

1½ pounds chicken drumsticks (about 4 drumsticks)

1½ teaspoons kosher salt

1 teaspoon freshly ground black pepper

1 tablespoon vegetable oil

Three ½-inch-thick slices from 1 white or yellow onion

4 large garlic cloves, sliced

1 California or guajillo chile, stemmed, seeded, and torn into pieces

1 Roma tomato, cored, seeded, and diced

¼ teaspoon dried Mexican oregano

1 cup chicken broth

1 whole clove

1 whole chipotle chile in adobo sauce, plus chopped chipotle chile, to taste

2 tablespoons chopped fresh cilantro leaves (optional)

You can do the little bit of prep for this speedy, simple chicken in the time it takes for the Instant Pot to heat up. Although I like to use drumsticks and bone-in, skin-on chicken thighs for flavor, you can substitute boneless thighs if you prefer. Serve with rice and a salad. Leftover chicken, if you have any, is terrific shredded and added to burritos.

Season the chicken thighs and drumsticks on all sides with the salt and pepper.

Press **Sauté—high** on the Instant Pot and heat the oil. Working in batches, add the chicken in a single layer and cook until well browned on both sides, about 4 minutes per side. Transfer the chicken to a plate.

Add the onion slices to the pot and cook without stirring for about 3 minutes, until golden brown. Turn the slices, then add the garlic, California chile, tomato, and oregano. Cook, stirring occasionally, for about 2 minutes, until the tomato softens a bit. Press **Cancel**. Pour in the broth and scrape up any browned bits on the bottom of the pot. Stir in the clove and whole chipotle chile. Return the chicken to the pot, arranging the pieces in an even layer, then pour in any accumulated juices.

Secure the lid and set the Pressure Release to **Sealing**. Press **Meat/Stew**, then set the cooking time for 20 minutes. When the cooking program is complete, press **Cancel**. Perform a quick pressure release by moving the Pressure Release to **Venting**. Open the pot and let cool for 10 minutes.

Using tongs, transfer the chicken to a large plate. Press **Sauté—high**. Place an immersion blender in the pot and puree the cooking liquid until smooth. Cook, stirring occasionally, for 5 to 7 minutes, until thickened and reduced to 2 cups. Taste for seasoning and add salt and chopped chipotle chile if needed. Return the chicken to the pot and pour in any accumulated juices. Cook for about 5 minutes, until the chicken is heated through. Sprinkle with the cilantro (if using) and serve.

CHICKEN BARBACOA

In Mexico, *barbacoa* is traditionally made with goat or lamb, which is cooked overnight in agave leaves with spices and aromatics. Here, the mildly spicy flavors of a traditional barbacoa are paired with boneless chicken thighs, cooked in an easy salsa. Serve with fresh limes, diced onions, and plenty of cilantro to spark up the flavor. Warm tortillas, rice, and beans and ice-cold beer are the essential accompaniments!

In a blender, combine the tomato, onion, garlic, ginger, ground chile, salt, pepper, and serrano chile. Blend until very smooth.

Press **Sauté—high** on the Instant Pot and heat the oil. Add the chicken in a single layer, cooking in batches if necessary, and cook until well browned on both sides, about 4 minutes per side. Transfer to a large plate.

Pour the tomato-chile puree into the pot and cook, stirring occasionally, for 3 to 5 minutes, until slightly thickened. Stir in the broth, beer, tequila, vinegar, and cilantro, scraping up any browned bits from the bottom of the pot. Return the chicken to the pot, arranging the pieces in an even layer, then pour in any accumulated juices. Press **Cancel**. Secure the lid and set the Pressure Release to **Sealing**. Press **Meat/Stew**, then set the cooking time for 15 minutes.

When the cooking program is complete, press **Cancel**. Perform a quick pressure release by moving the Pressure Release to **Venting**. Open the pot and let cool for about 15 minutes. Taste and adjust the seasoning with salt and pepper if needed.

Serve the barbacoa with warmed tortillas, rice, beans, lime wedges, diced onion, and cilantro on the side.

Serves 4 to 6

1 Roma tomato, cored and cut into quarters

½ cup diced white or yellow onion

2 garlic cloves, peeled

2 teaspoons minced fresh ginger

2 tablespoons guajillo or California chile powder

1 teaspoon kosher salt

1 teaspoon freshly ground black pepper

1 serrano chile, stemmed

2 tablespoons vegetable oil

2½ pounds boneless, skinless chicken thighs

½ cup chicken broth

¼ cup dark beer

1 tablespoon tequila

1 tablespoon cider vinegar

¼ cup minced fresh cilantro leaves

FOR SERVING

Warmed corn tortillas

Arroz Blanco (page 134)

Basic Black Beans (see Notes, page 23) or Cowboy Pinto Beans (page 129)

Limes wedges

Diced white onion

Chopped fresh cilantro leaves

CHICKEN DIABLA TACOS

Serves 4

3 Roma tomatoes, cored and cut into eighths

1 small white or yellow onion, roughly chopped

4 large garlic cloves, peeled

¼ cup chipotle chiles in adobo sauce, plus more if needed

1 tablespoon tomato paste

1 teaspoon kosher salt

1 teaspoon freshly ground black pepper

2 tablespoons vegetable oil

2½ pounds boneless, skinless chicken thighs or breasts

2 Anaheim chiles or green bell peppers, stemmed, seeded, and cut into ½-inch wide strips

2 tablespoons minced fresh cilantro leaves

Juice of 1 lime

FOR SERVING

Avocado slices

Taco Slaw (page 151)

Diced white onion

Chopped fresh cilantro

Shredded lettuce (optional)

Pico de Gallo (page 139; optional)

Warmed corn tortillas

Lime wedges

Once you've done the prep work, this dish comes together in about a half hour. You may have a little extra *salsa diabla*; save and freeze for another day. Or instead of making tacos, serve the chicken in pieces as a *platillo*, with lots of salsa, toppings, and a generous serving of rice. I like Arroz Blanco (page 134) or Arroz Verde (page 131), with diced avocado and onion on top, and Basic Black Beans (page 23) on the side.

In a blender, combine the tomatoes, onion, garlic, chipotle chiles, tomato paste, salt, and pepper. Blend until smooth, scraping down the blender as needed. Taste and blend in more chipotles if desired. (The spiciness dilutes with cooking.)

Press **Sauté—high** on the Instant Pot and heat the oil. Add the chicken in a single layer, cooking in batches if necessary, and cook until well browned on both sides, about 4 minutes per side. Transfer to a large plate. Pour in the tomato-chipotle puree and cook, scraping up any browned bits on the bottom of the pot and stirring occasionally, for about 5 minutes, until thickened. Stir in the Anaheim chiles, then return the chicken to the pot, arranging it in an even layer, and pour in any accumulated juices. Press **Cancel**.

Secure the lid and set the Pressure Release to **Sealing**. Press **Meat/Stew**, then set the cooking time for 15 minutes. When the cooking program is complete, press **Cancel**. Let the pressure release naturally for 15 minutes, then move the Pressure Release to **Venting** to release any remaining steam.

Open the pot. Using tongs, transfer the chicken to a cutting board, then using two forks, shred into 1-inch pieces. Return the chicken to the pot, stir in the cilantro and lime juice, taste, and adjust the seasoning with salt and pepper if needed. Serve the chicken with avocado, slaw, diced onion, cilantro, lettuce (if using), pico de gallo (if using), and tortillas for making tacos. Pass lime wedges on the side.

ACHIOTE CHICKEN TACOS

In this Caribbean slant on tacos, the marinade is permeated with the brick-red color and earthy, unique flavor of achiote paste. The tacos are topped with fresh-tasting mojo salsa, as well as crunchy Taco Slaw and sliced avocado. Serve with Refried Pinto Beans (page 124) or Basic Black Beans (page 23). Plan on marinating the chicken for at least 1 hour.

To make the chicken: In a bowl, combine the chipotles, garlic, achiote paste, orange juice, lime juice, vinegar, cumin, oregano, salt, and pepper. Using a fork, mash to a smooth paste. Add the chicken and stir until well coated on all sides. Cover and refrigerate for at least 1 hour, or up to overnight.

Press **Sauté—high** on the Instant Pot and heat the oil. Working in batches, remove the chicken from the marinade and add to the pot in a single layer, shaking off any excess marinade. Cook until well browned on both sides, about 4 minutes per side. Transfer to a large plate. If needed, press **Sauté—low** to lower the heat and avoid scorching. Press **Cancel**.

Pour 1 cup water into the Instant Pot, then place the long-handled wire rack in the pot. Place the chicken on the rack in an even layer, over the water.

Secure the lid and set the Pressure Release to **Sealing**. Press **Meat/Stew**, then set the cooking time for 15 minutes.

While the chicken cooks, make the salsa: In a bowl, stir together the onions, tomato, orange juice, lime juice, vinegar, cilantro, salt, and about half of the garlic. Taste and adjust the seasoning with additional garlic, vinegar, and salt if needed. The salsa should be assertively seasoned. Set aside.

CONTINUED

Serves 4

CHICKEN

¼ cup chipotle chiles in adobo sauce, minced

6 large garlic cloves, minced

3 tablespoons achiote paste (see page 9), crumbled

2 tablespoons fresh orange juice

2 tablespoons fresh lime juice

2 tablespoons white vinegar

2 teaspoons ground cumin

2 teaspoons dried Mexican oregano, rubbed between your fingers

2 teaspoons kosher salt

2 teaspoons freshly ground black pepper

2½ pounds boneless, skinless chicken thighs

2 tablespoons vegetable oil

MOJO SALSA

2 green onions, thinly sliced

½ Roma tomato, cored, seeded, and minced

2 tablespoons fresh orange juice

1 tablespoon fresh lime juice

½ teaspoon white vinegar, plus more if needed

1 tablespoon minced fresh cilantro

½ teaspoon kosher salt

1 small garlic clove, minced to a paste

When the cooking program is complete, press **Cancel**. Perform a quick pressure release by moving the Pressure Release to **Venting**. Open the pot, using tongs, transfer the chicken to a plate, tent with aluminum foil, and let rest for about 5 minutes.

Cut the chicken into thick slices and serve with the salsa, slaw, avocado, cilantro, onions, pepitas, and tortillas for making tacos.

FOR SERVING
Taco Slaw (page 151)
Avocado slices
Chopped cilantro
Diced white onions
Pepitas (shelled pumpkin seeds)
Warmed tortillas

CHICKEN SANGRIA

This a special dish, and one of my favorites. I found it in a nineteenth-century cookbook from central Mexico, and it demonstrates the Spanish influence on upper-class Mexican cooking of that era. The chicken soaks overnight in a wine and citrus marinade and is served with a quickly made sauce, spiked with pomegranate juice. The sweet and salty garnishes are the perfect finish. In season, scatter a few tart pomegranate seeds over the chicken just before serving.

To make the marinade: In a small saucepan, combine the wine, vinegar, peppercorns, coriander seeds, clove, bay, cinnamon, onion, orange slices, lemon slices, and salt. Bring to a boil, then turn off the heat, and let stand for 30 minutes to allow the flavors to infuse.

Place the chicken in a large bowl and pour the marinade on top. Cover with plastic wrap and refrigerate overnight.

Just before cooking, remove the chicken from the marinade and pat dry with paper towels. Pour the marinade through a wire-mesh strainer set over a bowl; discard the solids in the strainer.

Press **Sauté—high** on the Instant Pot and heat 1 tablespoon of the olive oil. Working in batches, add the chicken in a single layer and cook until well browned on both sides, about 4 minutes per side. Transfer to a large plate. After all the chicken has been browned, season the skin sides with the salt.

Add the strained marinade, the broth, pomegranate juice, and garlic to the pot. Bring to a boil and cook, scraping up any browned bits on the bottom of the pot, until reduced by about half, 3 to 5 minutes. Place the long-handled wire rack in the

CONTINUED

Serves 4

MARINADE
1 cup fruity red wine, such as Zinfandel or a Cabernet blend

1 tablespoon red wine vinegar

6 black peppercorns, crushed

6 coriander seeds, crushed

1 whole clove, crushed

½ bay leaf

One 1-inch piece Ceylon cinnamon stick, lightly crushed, or ¼ teaspoon ground cinnamon

Two 1-inch-thick slices from 1 white or red onion

Two 1-inch-thick orange slices

Two 1-inch-thick lemon slices

1 teaspoon kosher salt

3 pounds bone-in, skin-on chicken thighs (about 8 thighs)

1½ tablespoons olive oil

½ teaspoon kosher salt

1 cup chicken broth

¼ cup pomegranate juice

1 garlic clove, crushed and peeled

Three ¼-inch-thick orange slices

2 tablespoons raisins

4 large green olives, pitted and halved lengthwise

2 teaspoons butter (optional)

Instant Pot, then place the chicken skin side up on the rack in an even layer, over the cooking liquid.

Secure the lid and set the Pressure Release to **Sealing**. Press **Meat/Stew**, then set the cooking time for 20 minutes.

While chicken is cooking, in a medium skillet, heat the remaining 1½ teaspoons olive oil over medium heat. Add the orange slices and cook for about 1 minute, until lightly browned and softened. Transfer to a plate. Add the raisins to the skillet and cook, stirring, for about 1 minute, then add the olives and cook, stirring, for about 30 seconds more. Transfer to the plate with the orange slices. Reserve the skillet for reducing the sauce.

When the cooking program is complete, press **Cancel**. Perform a quick pressure release by moving the Pressure Release to **Venting**. Open the pot and let cool for 10 minutes.

Preheat the broiler with a rack positioned about 6 inches below the element.

Using tongs, transfer the chicken skin side up in a single layer to a broiler-safe serving dish. Pat the skin dry with paper towels, then broil for 4 to 6 minutes, until the skin is browned and crisp.

While the chicken broils, pour the cooking liquid through a wire-mesh strainer into the reserved skillet. Set the pan over high heat and cook until for 1 to 3 minutes, until the liquid thick, syrupy, and reduced to about ¾ cup. Stir in the butter (if using). Taste and adjust the seasoning with salt if needed.

Pour a small amount of the sauce around the chicken and top the chicken with the sautéed orange slices, raisins, and olives. Serve right away and offer the remaining the sauce on the side.

CHICKEN IN ANCHO CHILE SALSA

This recipe makes great use of the Instant Pot's versatility. The delicious Ancho Chile Salsa is made right in the pot, and the chicken is then cooked on top of it. You'll have plenty of extra salsa left over to use on a burrito, enchilada, or tamale.

Season the chicken on all sides with the salt.

Press **Sauté—high** on the Instant Pot and heat the oil. Working in batches, add the chicken in a single layer and cook until well browned on both sides, about 4 minutes per side. Transfer to a large plate.

Press **Cancel**. Pour in the salsa and return the chicken to the pot, arranging the pieces in an even layer, then pour in the accumulated juices.

Secure the lid and set the Pressure Release to **Sealing**. Press **Meat/Stew**, then set the cooking time for 20 minutes.

When the cooking program is complete, press **Cancel**. Perform a quick pressure release by moving the Pressure Release to **Venting**. Open the pot and let cool for 10 minutes.

Stir in 3 tablespoons of the cilantro. Press **Sauté—low** on the Instant Pot, bring the mixture to a simmer, and cook for about 5 minutes to incorporate the flavors. Taste and adjust the seasoning with salt if needed. Sprinkle with the remaining 1 tablespoon cilantro. Serve with rice and warmed tortillas.

NOTE If you prefer, you can use 2½ pounds boneless, skinless chicken instead of bone-in, skin-on parts. Reduce the cooking time to 15 minutes.

Serves 4 to 6

3½ pounds bone-in, skin-on chicken parts

1 teaspoon kosher salt

2 tablespoons vegetable oil

1 recipe Ancho Chile Salsa (page 146)

4 tablespoons chopped fresh cilantro leaves

Arroz Blanco (page 134) for serving

Warmed corn or flour tortillas for serving

CHIPOTLE-LIME ROASTED CHICKEN

Serves 4

One 3 - to 4-pound whole chicken

3 teaspoons kosher salt

9 garlic cloves, peeled (about 3 tablespoons)

¼ cup chipotle chiles in adobo sauce

2 tablespoons fresh lime juice

1 teaspoon olive oil

¾ cup chicken broth

1 tablespoon cornstarch

2 tablespoons white wine

¼ cup chopped fresh cilantro leaves

Lime wedges for serving

Yes, you can roast a whole chicken in the Instant Pot! It doesn't brown, but after cooking, simply run it under the broiler to get a nice crispy finish—a good hack for anything you want to brown or crisp up. During cooking, the foil keeps the breast moist. Serve with Papas con Crema y Chiles (page 109).

Season the chicken inside and out with 2 teaspoons of the salt. Place on a large plate, cover, and refrigerate for about 1 hour.

Using a small food processor or mortar and pestle, puree the garlic, chipotle chiles, lime juice, oil, and the remaining 1 teaspoon salt to a smooth paste. Divide the paste evenly between two small bowls.

Using paper towels, wipe the chicken dry, inside and out. Rub the outside of the chicken with half of the chipotle paste, then, using kitchen twine, tie the legs together and tuck the wing tips behind the back.

Pour the broth into the Instant Pot. Place a long-handled wire rack in the pot and set the chicken breast up on the rack. Cut a 6-inch square of aluminum foil or parchment paper and place it on the breast to help protect it from overcooking.

Secure the lid and set the Pressure Release to **Sealing**. Press **Meat/Stew**, then set the cooking time for 20 minutes.

When the cooking program is complete, press **Cancel**. Perform a quick pressure release by moving the Pressure Release to **Venting**.

Open the pot. Wearing heat-resistant mitts, grasp the rack's handles and carefully lift the chicken out of the pot, setting it on a large plate. Remove and discard the foil from the breast. Let cool for about 5 minutes. Leave the cooking liquid in the Instant Pot.

Preheat the broiler with a rack positioned about 6 inches below the element.

Transfer the chicken to a cutting board. Cut the chicken in half with a large, sharp knife by first cutting down through the breastbone, then on both sides of the backbone. Remove the backbone. Place the halves skin side up on a broiler pan, then brush with the reserved chipotle paste. Broil for 4 to 6 minutes, until browned. Transfer the chicken to a warmed serving platter.

While chicken is broiling, press **Sauté—high** on the Instant Pot. Bring the cooking liquid to a boil and cook for about 2 minutes, until thickened. In a small bowl, stir together the cornstarch and wine, then whisk the mixture into the cooking liquid, along with any accumulated juices from the chicken. Bring to a simmer, stirring constantly, and cook for about 1 minute, until thickened. Taste and adjust the seasoning with salt if needed. Pour the sauce through a fine-mesh strainer into a warmed sauceboat or small bowl.

Sprinkle the chicken with the cilantro and serve with the sauce and lime wedges on the side.

ARROZ CON POLLO

Serves 4 to 6

1½ cups chicken broth

1 teaspoon saffron threads

3 pounds bone-in, skin-on chicken parts, or 2 pounds boneless, skinless chicken thighs

3 teaspoons kosher salt

1 teaspoon freshly ground black pepper

1 teaspoon red pepper flakes

2 tablespoons olive oil

1 small white or red onion, diced

4 large cloves garlic, minced

1 Anaheim chile, stemmed, seeded, and diced

2 Roma tomatoes, cored and diced, or one 14½-ounce can diced tomatoes, drained

1 teaspoon ground cumin

1 teaspoon smoked paprika

1 bay leaf

2 cups long-grain white rice, rinsed and drained

Reminiscent of paella but much faster and easier, this recipe makes the most delicious rice ever. It is infused with the flavors of chicken and a mix of spices, including saffron, which turns the dish golden. Serve with a simple salad.

In a small saucepan, bring ½ cup of the chicken broth to a bare simmer over medium-high heat. Add the saffron threads to the hot broth and let steep for about 30 minutes.

Season the chicken pieces on all sides with 1 teaspoon of the salt, the black pepper, and the pepper flakes. Press **Sauté—high** on the Instant Pot and heat the oil. Working in batches, add the chicken in a single layer and cook until well browned on both sides, about 4 minutes per side. Transfer to a large plate.

Add onion, garlic, and chile to the pot and cook, stirring occasionally, for about 2 minutes, until the onion begins to soften. Stir in the tomatoes, cumin, smoked paprika, bay leaf, and the remaining 2 teaspoon salt. Cook, stirring occasionally, for about 2 minutes, until the tomatoes have softened. Stir in the saffron-infused broth and the remaining 1 cup broth, scraping up any browned bit on the bottom of the pot. Press **Cancel**. Stir in the rice and, using a wooden spoon, gently swirl the rice until it falls into an even layer. Return the chicken to the pot, arranging the pieces in an even layer, then pour in any accumulated juices.

Secure the lid and set the Pressure Release to **Sealing**. Press **Meat/Stew**, then set the cooking time for 20 minutes.

When the cooking program is complete, press **Cancel**. Let the pressure release naturally for 10 minutes, then move the Pressure Release to **Venting** to release any remaining steam. Open the pot and let cool for 10 minutes to allow the rice to firm up, then serve.

TEQUILA-BRINED TURKEY

Serves 6 to 8

BRINE

2 tablespoons coriander seeds, crushed

1 tablespoon black peppercorns, crushed

1 tablespoon cumin seeds

1 tablespoon dried Mexican oregano

2 bay leaves, crumbled

8 cups water

1 cup kosher salt

½ cup packed brown sugar

¼ cup granulated sugar

½ cup blanco tequila or mezcal

One 3- to 4-pound skinless, bone-in turkey breast half, or 3 to 4 pounds skinless, bone-in turkey thighs

2 chipotle chiles in adobo sauce, minced to a paste

1 tablespoon fresh lime juice

1 large garlic clove, minced to a paste

1 cup chicken broth

2 tablespoons white wine

2 teaspoons cornstarch

1 tablespoon vegetable oil

Coriander seeds, peppercorns, and cumin seeds are browned right in the Instant Pot for the tequila-laced marinade that the turkey breast soaks in overnight. A chipotle rub, which goes on the turkey right before cooking, deepens its flavor. This is terrific with Quinoa con Pasas (page 135) and Corn Esquites (page 105). Or use the meat in place of chicken in soups, mole, tacos, or tamales.

———————————

To make the brine: Press **Sauté—normal/medium** on the Instant Pot. Add the coriander seeds, peppercorns, cumin seeds, oregano, and bay. Toast, stirring, for about 1 minute. Add the water, salt, brown sugar, and granulated sugar. Bring to a boil and cook, stirring to dissolve the salt and sugar, for about 5 minutes. Press **Cancel**.

Wearing heat-resistant mitts, lift the inner pot out of the Instant Pot housing. Let the brine cool in the inner pot for about 30 minutes, then stir in the tequila.

With a metal skewer, poke the turkey on all sides, spacing the holes about 2 inches apart; this will allow the brine to penetrate. Put the turkey into an extra-large ziplock plastic bag, then pour in the cooled brine. Seal the bag, pressing out as much air as possible. Refrigerate for at least 12 hours or for up to 24 hours.

In a small bowl, stir together the chipotle chiles, lime juice, and garlic. Pour the broth into the Instant Pot, then place the long-handled wire rack in the pot. Remove the turkey from the brine and pat dry with paper towels. Rub the turkey all over with the chipotle mixture, then set it on the rack. Lay a sheet of aluminum foil on top of the turkey and tuck the edges into the pot. Press **Poultry**, then set the cooking time for 30 minutes.

When the cooking program is complete, press **Cancel**. Perform a quick pressure release by moving the Pressure Release to **Venting**. Open the pot. Using tongs, transfer the turkey to a foil-lined sheet tray, cover with foil, and let rest for 20 minutes.

Meanwhile, remove the rack from the Instant Pot, then press **Sauté—normal/ medium**. In a small bowl, stir together the wine and cornstarch, then whisk the mixture into cooking liquid in the pot. Whisking constantly, bring to a simmer and cook for about 2 minutes, until thickened. Pour the sauce into a serving bowl and cover with foil to keep warm.

After the turkey has rested, preheat the broiler with a rack positioned about 4 inches below the element. Broil the turkey for 7 to 10 minutes, until golden brown.

Transfer the turkey to a cutting board and carve into slices. Serve with the sauce on the side.

DUCK LEG "CANARDITAS" WITH BLACKBERRY-MEZCAL SALSA

Serves 6

DUCK LEGS

¼ cup plus 2 teaspoons kosher salt

1 tablespoon plus 1 teaspoon crushed black peppercorns

4 garlic cloves, minced to a paste (1 tablespoon), plus 2 large garlic cloves, sliced

1 green onion, white and green parts, minced, or 1 shallot, minced

6 large duck legs (12 to 14 ounces each)

1 tablespoon vegetable oil

Two ½-inch-thick slices from 1 white or yellow onion

1 bay leaf

4 cups chicken broth

BLACKBERRY-MEZCAL SALSA

½ cup fresh blackberries

1 serrano chile, stemmed and minced (with seeds)

1½ tablespoons fresh lime juice

2 teaspoons red wine vinegar, plus more if needed

2 teaspoons mezcal, tequila, or Grand Marnier

1 teaspoon minced fresh ginger

1 teaspoon sugar, plus more if needed

¾ teaspoon kosher salt

This modern variation on duck confit is made easier in the Instant Pot. But you need to allow at least a day to season the duck legs, cook them, and cool completely in the stock. A few minutes under the broiler yields a crisp skin to complement the moist, succulent meat. Serve as an entrée, or shred the meat and roll in tacos. The salsa is a spin on a classic French sauce for duck. Its strong and spicy flavor is balanced by its sweetness and acidity.

To prepare the duck legs: In a small bowl, stir together the salt, 1 tablespoon of the peppercorns, the garlic paste, and green onion. Using paper towels, wipe the duck legs dry, then rub all of the salt mixture into the flesh and skin. Place in a ziplock plastic freezer bag, seal the bag, and refrigerate for at least 12 hours or up to 1 day.

Rinse the duck legs thoroughly to remove all of the salt mixture, then set aside. Press **Sauté—normal/medium** on the Instant Pot and heat the oil. Add the onion, the sliced garlic, the bay, and the remaining 1 teaspoon peppercorns and cook, stirring occasionally, for about 6 minutes, until the onion has softened. Press **Cancel**. Pour in the broth, then place the duck legs skin side up in the pot so they won't stick to the sides or bottom of the pot.

Secure the lid and set the Pressure Release to **Sealing**. Press **Meat/Stew**, then set the cooking time for 20 minutes.

While the duck legs cook, make the salsa: Chop the blackberries until they're reduced to a pulp and place in a small bowl. Stir in the serrano, lime juice, vinegar, mezcal, ginger, sugar, and salt. Taste and adjust the seasoning with mezcal, vinegar, sugar, and salt if needed—the salsa should be quite spicy but balanced with sweetness and vinegar. Set aside.

When the cooking program is complete, press **Cancel**. Perform a quick pressure release by moving the Pressure Release to **Venting**. Open the pot and let cool for 45 minutes to 1 hour.

Using tongs, carefully transfer the duck legs, meat side up, to a foil-lined sheet tray. Pat both sides dry with paper towels, then turn the legs skin side down. (The cooking liquid can be strained, defatted, and reserved for another use. It can take the place of chicken broth in any recipe.)

Preheat the broiler with a rack positioned about 6 inches below the element. Broil the duck for about 5 minutes, until heated through. Using tongs, flip the duck legs skin side up and broil for 3 to 5 minutes, until the skin is crisp and golden. Serve right away with the salsa on the side.

ENCHILADAS

At their very simplest, enchiladas are corn tortillas lightly fried, dipped in a salsa, rolled, and eaten with a sprinkle of cotija cheese and maybe some onions on top. The filling is optional. An awesome enchilada is all that wrapped around a delicious filling and more salsa, sprinkled with extra cheese, and baked and served to your adoring audience with sour cream and crunchy onions. The *very best* enchiladas are assembled from hot ingredients and popped just briefly in the oven or under the broiler to bubble and brown.

The Instant Pot makes it easy to have enchiladas whenever you like! Juicy fillings and salsas are a snap to make and, with a little planning, can be prepared ahead of time and refrigerated or even frozen. Enchiladas are also an excellent way to use up any leftovers.

Enchiladas are typically rolled but can be simply folded (the lazy method). The truly lazy dip the tortillas in salsa and layer them with cheese and filling to make stacked enchiladas. These look great baked and served in individual dishes. It's not necessary to fry the tortillas; they can be warmed in a pan and rolled around the filling, but they may break apart and will be very soft after baking. They will still taste great, though.

Red Chile Salsa (page 141) and Salsa Verde (page 140) are the most common enchilada salsas, but consider experimenting with mole (see page 34) to make *enmoladas*, or thinned refried pinto beans (page 124) to make *enfrijoladas*. Enchiladas are typically not spicy, but you can provide hot sauce for those who love heat. See Enchilada Embellishments (page 59) for more suggestions.

CHICKEN AND CHEESE ENCHILADAS WITH SALSA VERDE

Serves 4

Shredded chicken from
1 recipe Uno-Dos-Tres
Shredded Chicken and Broth
(page 154), or 3 cups cooked,
shredded chicken (such as
rotisserie chicken)

3½ cups shredded Monterey
Jack cheese

Sixteen 6-inch corn tortillas

Vegetable oil for brushing
the tortillas

Salsa Verde (page 140)

½ cup diced white onion

¼ cup chopped fresh
cilantro leaves

½ cup Mexican crema

Garnishes of your choice (see
Enchilada Embellishments,
page 59) for serving

1 In a bowl, toss together the chicken and 2 cups of the cheese to make the filling.

2 Lightly brush the tortillas on both sides with oil. Heat a skillet over medium heat. One at a time, warm the tortillas for about 1 minute on each side, just until softened. Transfer to a plate, stacking the tortillas as they are done.

3 Preheat the oven to 350°F. Lightly grease a 9 by 13-inch baking dish with vegetable oil.

4 Spread ½ cup of the salsa in the bottom of the prepared baking dish. Place another ½ cup of the salsa in a pie plate. Have the tortillas, the salsa in the pie plate, the filling, and the baking dish all ready in an assembly line.

5 Quickly dip one side of a tortilla in the salsa in the pie plate. Lay the tortilla on your work surface with the salsa side facing down. Spoon about ⅓ cup of the filling across the center of the tortilla, then roll up tightly and place seam side down in the baking dish. Repeat with remaining tortillas, the remaining salsa for dipping the tortillas, and the remaining filling.

6 Spoon the remaining salsa evenly over the enchiladas, along with any salsa left in the pie plate. Sprinkle the remaining 1½ cups cheese over the top. Bake uncovered for 20 to 25 minutes, until the cheese is melted and bubbly.

7 Meanwhile, in a small bowl, stir together the onion and cilantro.

8 Remove the baking dish from the oven, then drizzle the hot enchiladas with crema and scatter the onion-cilantro mixture over the top. Serve right away with the garnishes of your choice.

FOUR-CHEESE ENCHILADAS
WITH TWO SALSAS

Serves 4

In a bowl, toss together 2 cups of the Jack cheese, the cream cheese, queso fresco, and epazote to make the filling.

Follow step 2 of Chicken and Cheese Enchiladas with Salsa Verde (facing page) to brush the tortillas with oil and warm them.

Follow steps 3 and 4 of Chicken and Cheese Enchiladas to preheat the oven and prepare the baking dish and assembly line.

Follow step 5 of Chicken and Cheese Enchiladas to fill the tortillas.

With the baking dish positioned perpendicular to the counter's edge, cover the left third of the enchiladas with the remaining salsa verde, along with any salsa left in the pie plate. Cover the center third with the remaining ½ cup Jack cheese, then top evenly with the sour cream. Cover the right third of the enchiladas with the red chile salsa. Bake uncovered for 20 to 25 minutes, until the cheese is melted and bubbly.

Meanwhile, in a small bowl, stir together the onion and cilantro.

Remove the baking dish from the oven, then sprinkle the cotija cheese down the center of the green and red stripes and scatter the onion-cilantro mixture down the white stripe. Serve right away, with the garnishes of your choice.

2½ cups shredded Monterey Jack cheese

½ cup cream cheese, cut into ¼-inch cubes

2 cups crumbled queso fresco

⅓ cup shredded fresh epazote leaves or chopped fresh cilantro leaves

Twelve 6-inch corn tortillas

Vegetable oil for brushing the tortillas

1½ cups Salsa Verde (page 140)

½ cup sour cream

1½ cups Red Chile Salsa (page 141)

½ cup diced white onion

½ cup chopped fresh cilantro leaves

⅓ cup grated cotija cheese

Garnishes of your choice (see Enchilada Embellishments, page 59) for serving

BEEF AND BEAN ENCHILADAS

Serves 4 to 6

FILLING

1 tablespoon vegetable oil

⅓ cup diced white onion

1 small garlic clove, minced

2 Roma tomatoes, cored, seeded, and diced

½ teaspoon ground cumin

1 teaspoon kosher salt

½ teaspoon freshly ground black pepper

Shredded beef plus ½ cup broth from Uno-Dos-Tres Shredded Beef and Broth (page 156)

1 cup Cowboy Pinto Beans (page 129), hot

⅓ cup chopped fresh cilantro leaves

2 cups Red Chile Salsa (page 141)

Vegetable oil for brushing the tortillas

Twelve 6-inch corn tortillas

1½ cups shredded pepper Jack cheese

⅓ cup diced white onion

¼ cup chopped fresh cilantro leaves

½ cup Mexican crema

Garnishes of your choice (see Enchilada Embellishments, facing page)

Habanero hot sauce (page 144)

To make the filling: In a skillet over medium-high heat, warm the oil. Add the onion, garlic, tomatoes, cumin, salt, and pepper. Cook, stirring, for about 1 minute. Add the beef and broth and cook, stirring occasionally, for about 5 minutes, until almost dry. Fold in the beans and cilantro and remove from the heat.

Follow step 2 of Chicken and Cheese Enchiladas with Salsa Verde (page 56) to brush the tortillas with oil and warm them.

Follow steps 3 and 4 of Chicken and Cheese Enchiladas to preheat the oven and prepare the baking dish and assembly line.

Follow step 5 of Chicken and Cheese Enchiladas to fill the tortillas.

Spoon the remaining 1 cup salsa evenly over the enchiladas, along with any salsa left in the pie plate. Sprinkle the cheese over the top. Bake uncovered for 15 to 20 minutes, until cheese is melted and bubbly.

Meanwhile, in a small bowl, stir together the onion and cilantro.

Remove the baking dish from the oven, then drizzle the crema over the enchiladas and scatter the onion-cilantro mixture over the top. Serve right away, with the garnishes of your choice and the hot sauce.

MUSHROOM ENCHILADAS WITH CHEESY CHIPOTLE SAUCE

Follow step 2 of Chicken and Cheese Enchiladas with Salsa Verde (page 56) to brush the tortillas with oil and warm them.

Preheat the broiler with a rack positioned about 4 inches below the element. Lightly grease a broiler-safe 9 by 13-inch baking dish.

Fill each tortilla with about ¼ cup of the mushroom filling, then fold the tortilla in half and place in the prepared baking dish. Overlap the tortillas slightly so that they all fit.

Spoon the chipotle sauce evenly over the enchiladas, then sprinkle with the cotija cheese and green onions. Broil for 2 to 4 minutes, until the sauce starts to bubble and brown. Serve right away with the garnishes of your choice.

Serves 4

Twelve 6-inch corn tortillas

Vegetable oil for brushing the tortillas

Mushroom filling from Mushroom "Quesotacos" with Epazote (page 110), hot

1 recipe Cheesy Chipotle Sauce (page 147), hot

⅓ cup grated cotija cheese

2 green onions, green parts only, thinly sliced

Garnishes of your choice (see Enchilada Embellishments, below) for serving

ENCHILADA EMBELLISHMENTS

Here are some garnishes that are terrific alongside enchiladas of any type:

- Habanero hot sauce (page 144)
- Pico de Gallo (page 139)
- Pickled jalapeños, homemade (see page 149) or store-bought
- Guacamole (page 150)

chapter 3

BEEF
&
PORK

MEXICO CITY SHORT RIBS WITH POBLANO CHILES

Serves 4

2 tablespoons vegetable oil

2 pounds boneless beef short ribs, trimmed of fat and cut into 2-inch pieces

1 small white or yellow onion, diced

4 garlic cloves, minced

2 teaspoons kosher salt

½ teaspoon freshly ground black pepper

½ teaspoon ground cumin

¼ teaspoon ground cinnamon

1 whole clove

1 bay leaf

1 Roma tomato, cored and chopped to pulp

½ cup Red Chile Salsa (page 141) or store-bought red enchilada sauce

½ cup dark beer, such as Negra Modelo, or beef stock

2 poblano chiles, roasted (see page 6), peeled, seeded, and diced

4 teaspoons masa harina

FOR SERVING

Diced white onion

Chopped fresh cilantro leaves

Warmed corn or flour tortillas

Arroz Blanco (page 134)

Sour cream (optional)

This rather elegant take on a simple beef *guisado* gets its zip from the beer and roasted poblano chiles. It's thickened with masa harina, but you can use corn tortillas in a pinch (see Notes). Use roasted Anaheim chiles instead of poblanos for less heat, or roasted Hatch chiles if you want even more. The short ribs make a terrific burrito (see page 120).

Press **Sauté—high** on the Instant Pot and heat the oil. Working in batches, add the beef in a single layer and cook until well browned on all sides, about 2 minutes per side. Transfer to a large plate. Add the onion and garlic and cook, stirring, for about 1 minute. Add the salt, pepper, cumin, cinnamon, clove, and bay. Cook, stirring frequently, for about 2 minutes. Press **Cancel**.

Return the beef to the pot, then stir in the tomato, salsa, and beer. Secure the lid and set the Pressure Release to **Sealing**. Press **Meat/Stew**, then set the cooking time for 25 minutes.

When the cooking program is complete, press **Cancel**. Let the pressure release naturally for 30 minutes, then move the Pressure Release to **Venting** to release any remaining steam.

Open the pot, then press **Sauté—high**. Stir in the poblano chiles and masa harina. Bring to a simmer and cook, stirring occasionally, for about 5 minutes, until thickened. Serve topped with diced onion and cilantro and with tortillas, rice, and sour cream (if using) on the side.

NOTES If you like, substitute boneless beef chuck roast, cut into 2-inch pieces, for the short ribs.

If you don't have masa harina, soak 2 small corn tortillas in stock or water until moistened, then puree in a blender. Use the puree as you would the masa harina.

RED CHILE BEEF STEW

This classic *charro* (cowboy) stew from northern Mexico is ready in less than an hour, if you have some Red Chile Salsa stashed in your freezer. The masa dumplings are substantial enough to be served in place of rice (see Variation). The stew is terrific in burritos (see page 117), tamales (see page 93), and enchiladas (see page 55), and served as a taco.

Serves 4

1 tablespoon vegetable oil

2 pounds boneless beef chuck roast or top round, cut into 1-inch pieces

1 large white or yellow onion, cut into ½-inch dice

6 garlic cloves, minced

1 teaspoon ground cumin or cumin

½ teaspoon dried Mexican oregano

1 whole clove

½ teaspoon freshly ground black pepper

2 Roma tomatoes, cored and roughly chopped (about 1 cup)

1 cup beef broth

1 cup Red Chile Salsa (page 141)

½ cup dark beer, such as Negra Modelo, or beef stock (optional)

2 teaspoons masa harina, or one 6-inch corn tortilla, torn into small pieces

Leaves from ¼ bunch cilantro, roughly chopped

Cowboy Pinto Beans (page 129) for serving

Arroz Blanco (page 134) or Arroz Rojo (page 127) for serving

Press **Sauté—high** on the Instant Pot and heat the oil. Working in batches, add the beef in a single layer and cook, turning as needed, for about 10 minutes, until well browned on all sides. Add the onion, garlic, cumin, oregano, and spices and cook, stirring, for about 2 minutes. Press **Cancel**. Stir in the tomatoes, broth, salsa, and beer (if using).

Secure the lid and set the Pressure Release to **Sealing**. Press **Meat/Stew**, then set the cooking time for 20 minutes.

When the cooking program is complete, press **Cancel**. Let the pressure release naturally for 30 minutes, then move the Pressure Release to **Venting** to release any remaining steam. Open the pot and press **Sauté—high**. Stir in the masa harina, bring to a simmer, and cook, stirring occasionally, for about 10 minutes, until the sauce is thickened and the meat is falling apart. Taste and adjust the seasoning with salt if needed, then stir in the cilantro. Serve with the beans and rice.

VARIATION

For Red Chile Beef Stew with Masa Dumplings, while the stew is cooking, in a bowl, whisk together ¼ cup warm whole milk and 1 tablespoon melted butter. Whisk in 1 large egg and 1 teaspoon kosher salt until well combined. Add ⅓ cup Maseca brand masa harina and stir with a fork until a soft but not sticky dough forms. With moistened hands, pinch off a roughly 1-inch ball of the dough and flatten it between your thumb and index finger, indenting both sides. Set on a large plate. Repeat with the remaining dough. You should have about 12 dumplings. Add the dumplings to the stew in place of the masa harina and cook for about 5 minutes, until the dumplings are firm.

STEAK FAJITAS WITH CHIMICHURRI

Fajitas, or *carne estofado* as it sometimes called, is usually cooked like a stir-fry in a round pan called a *disco*. This Instant Pot version combines quick-braised beef strips with crunchy vegetables in a couple of easy steps. The flavor of the fajitas is enhanced by an overnight soak in a marinade and a dash of chimichurri. Serve with Arroz Rojo (page 127).

To marinate the steak: Using a sharp chef's knife, slice the meat into ½-inch-wide strips (if using flank steak, make sure to cut against the grain). Add to a large bowl along with the soy sauce, lime juice, garlic, salt, black pepper, and pepper flakes. Toss to combine, then cover and refrigerate for at least 30 minutes or up to overnight.

Press **Sauté—normal/medium** on the Instant Pot and heat the oil. Add the onion and garlic and cook, stirring occasionally, for about 5 minutes, until the onion is translucent. Add the red bell pepper, poblano chiles, jalapeños, and tomato and cook, stirring occasionally, for 3 to 5 minutes, until the vegetables are crisp-tender. Transfer to a large plate, season with the salt, and set aside.

Working in batches, add the beef in a single, uncrowded layer to the Instant Pot and cook until well browned on both sides, about 2 minutes per side, without stirring; reserve any remaining marinade. Transfer the browned beef to another large plate and set aside. Press **Cancel**.

Pour the broth into the pot and, using a wooden spoon, scape up any browned bits from the bottom of the pot. Return 1 cup of the cooked vegetables to the pot, setting the rest aside. Place the beef in an even layer on top of the vegetables, then pour in the reserved marinade.

CONTINUED

Serves 4

MARINATED STEAK
One 2-pound beef top round steak or flank steak

2 tablespoons soy sauce

1 tablespoon fresh lime juice

8 large garlic cloves, minced

2 teaspoons kosher salt

2 teaspoons freshly ground black pepper

½ teaspoon red pepper flakes

1 tablespoon vegetable oil

1 red onion, halved and sliced lengthwise into ½-inch-wide strips

4 large garlic cloves, sliced

1 small red bell pepper, stemmed, seeded, and cut into ½-inch-wide strips

2 poblano or Anaheim chiles, stemmed, seeded, and cut into ½-inch-wide strips

2 jalapeño chiles, stemmed, seeded, and cut into strips

1 Roma tomato, cored, seeded, and cut lengthwise into ½-inch-wide strips

1 teaspoon kosher salt

¼ cup beef broth

CHIMICHURRI

¼ cup olive oil

4 garlic cloves, minced to a paste

2 teaspoons fresh lime juice

2 teaspoons finely minced white or red onion or green onion tops

1 teaspoon black peppercorns, crushed with a large, sharp knife, or 1 teaspoon freshly ground black pepper

¼ teaspoon kosher salt

¼ teaspoon red pepper flakes

Leaves from 6 large sprigs flat-leaf parsley, minced

Leaves from 6 large sprigs cilantro, minced

FOR SERVING

Chopped fresh cilantro leaves

Avocado slices

Warmed corn or flour tortillas

Lime wedges

Secure the lid and set the Pressure Release to **Sealing**. Press **Meat/Stew**, then set the cooking time for 20 minutes.

While the steak cooks, make the chimichurri: In a small bowl, stir together all of the ingredients. Cover and set aside at room temperature until ready to serve.

When the cooking program is complete, press **Cancel**. Perform a quick pressure release by moving the Pressure Release to **Venting**. Open the pot and, using a slotted spoon, transfer the beef and vegetables to a serving platter, then cover with aluminum foil to keep warm.

Press **Sauté—high** on the Instant Pot. Bring the cooking liquid to a boil and cook until reduced to 1 cup, 5 to 7 minutes. Stir in the reserved vegetables and beef and cook for about 1 minute, just until heated through, and transfer to the serving platter. Serve the fajitas with the cilantro, avocado, chimichurri, and tortillas for filling. Pass lime wedges on the side.

VARIATION

For Chicken Fajitas with Chimichurri, substitute 2 pounds boneless, skinless chicken thighs for the steak and reduce the cooking time to 15 minutes.

MEXICAN MEAT LOAF

Topped with strips of poblano chile and melted Mexican cheese, this is no ordinary meat loaf. The chorizo and other aromatics are cooked in the Instant Pot to bring out their flavors before mixing them into the meat. No need for a pan for the meat loaf; form the meat into a loaf shape and wrap in foil to keep in all the juices. It will taste even better the next day.

Press **Sauté—normal/medium** on the Instant Pot and heat the oil. Add the onion, chile, and garlic and cook, stirring occasionally, for about 5 minutes, until the onion is translucent. Add the chorizo and cook, stirring occasionally, for about 10 minutes, until the chorizo is no longer pink. Press **Cancel**. Transfer the chorizo mixture to a bowl and let cool to room temperature.

Cut a 16-inch length of aluminum foil. In a large bowl, combine the ground beef, ground pork, salt, pepper, egg white, cooked rice, tomato paste, and cilantro. Add the cooled chorizo mixture and mix with your hands until the ingredients are evenly distributed. Transfer the mixture to the foil and form it into a loaf about 4 inches wide, 4 inches tall, and 6 inches long. Fold up the edges of the foil and crimp them to enclose the loaf.

Pour 1½ cups water into the Instant Pot, then place the long-handled wire rack in the pot. Place the loaf on top. Secure the lid and set the Pressure Release to **Sealing**. Press **Meat/Stew**, then set the cooking time for 30 minutes.

When the cooking program is complete, press **Cancel**. Perform a quick pressure release by moving the Pressure Release to **Venting**. Open the pot, then insert an instant-read thermometer through the foil into the center of the meat loaf. It should register 165°F. If it does not, once again secure the lid and set the Pressure

CONTINUED

Serves 4

1 tablespoon vegetable oil

½ Anaheim chile or green bell pepper, finely diced (½ cup)

1 small white or yellow onion, finely diced

3 garlic cloves, minced

8 ounces Mexican-style chorizo sausage, casing removed, crumbled

1 pound ground beef (80% lean)

8 ounces ground pork

1 teaspoon kosher salt

1 teaspoon freshly ground black pepper

1 large egg white

½ cup cooked rice (any kind), or 2 tablespoons ground oats

1 tablespoon plus 1 teaspoon tomato paste

2 tablespoons chopped fresh cilantro leaves

1 large poblano chile, roasted (see page 6), seeded, peeled, and cut into 1-inch-wide strips

⅔ cup shredded Monterey Jack cheese (optional)

Tomatillo-Chipotle Salsa (page 142) or Salsa Ranchera (page 152) for serving

Release to **Sealing**. Press **Meat/Stew**, then set the cooking time for 5 minutes. When the cooking program is complete, press **Cancel**. Perform a quick pressure release by moving the Pressure Release to **Venting**. Open the pot, then let the meat loaf rest in the pot for 5 minutes.

While the meat loaf rests, preheat the broiler with a rack positioned about 8 inches below the element.

Wearing heat-resistant mitts, grasp the rack's handles and carefully lift the meat loaf out of the pot. Carefully unwrap the hot meat loaf and transfer to an oven-proof platter. Lay the strips of poblano chile across the top, then sprinkle evenly with the cheese (if using). Broil for 5 to 7 minutes, until the cheese is bubbly, or if not using cheese, until the top of the loaf starts to get crispy and browned.

Cut the meat loaf into slices and serve with the salsa.

NOTES Add 1 cup cooked corn kernels or 2 cups finely shredded kale to the meat mixture before forming into a loaf.

Instead of forming the meat loaf on foil, press the meat mixture into a greased 7-inch round cake pan, a 6-inch loaf pan, or a 1-quart Bundt pan. Cover with foil and cook as directed, then unmold before broiling.

PORK AND LONGANIZA STEW
WITH BEANS AND KALE

Think of this dish as a Latin version of the French cassoulet, featuring Mexican *longaniza*, a flavorful garlic sausage (if you can't find *longanizas* at a Mexican grocery store, fresh garlic sausages may be substituted). I recommend presoaking the beans overnight so the meat doesn't overcook before the beans are done. The stew will be brothy at first, so be sure to let it rest, and it will thicken up nicely.

Place the beans in a large bowl, cover with 4 cups water, and let soak overnight at room temperature. Drain the beans.

Press **Sauté—normal/medium** on the Instant Pot and heat 1 tablespoon of the oil. Add the onion, garlic, ancho chile, and árbol chile and cook, stirring occasionally, for about 10 minutes, until the onion is golden brown. Transfer to a plate.

Add the remaining 1 tablespoon oil and the sausage to the pot. Cook, stirring occasionally, for about 5 minutes, until the sausage is no longer pink. Add the pork and cook, stirring occasionally, for about 5 minutes, until lightly browned. Add the drained beans, marjoram, bay, salt, pepper, water, and tomatoes, then stir to combine. Press **Cancel**. Secure the lid and set the Pressure Release to **Sealing**. Press **Meat/Stew**, then set the cooking time for 25 minutes.

Meanwhile, bring a large saucepan of salted water to a boil over high heat. Add the greens and cook for 2 minutes. Drain in a colander and set aside.

When the cooking program is complete, press **Cancel**. Let the pressure release naturally for 10 minutes, then move the Pressure Release to **Venting** to release any remaining pressure. Open the pot and stir in the greens; the stew will be brothy but will thicken as it rests. Replace the lid without securing it and let stand for 10 minutes. Taste and adjust the seasoning with salt and pepper if needed. Serve topped with chicharrón (if using).

Serves 6

1 cup dried Great Northern beans

2 tablespoons vegetable oil or fresh lard (see page 10)

1 large white or yellow onion, diced

6 garlic cloves, sliced

1 ancho chile, stemmed, seeded, and torn into pieces

1 chile de árbol, stemmed and seeded

12 ounces longaniza sausage, casing removed, broken into small chunks

1 pound boneless pork shoulder, cut into 1-inch pieces

½ teaspoon dried marjoram

1 bay leaf

2 teaspoons kosher salt

1 teaspoon freshly ground black pepper

3 cups water, beef broth, or chicken broth

3 Roma tomatoes, cored and diced (about 1½ cups), or one 14½-ounce can diced tomatoes, drained

1 bunch kale, Swiss chard, or collard greens, stemmed and cut into ½-inch-wide ribbons

½ cup crumbled chicharrón (optional)

BEEF MACHACA TACOS

Serves 4 to 6

3 tablespoons vegetable oil

½ red onion, sliced

2 large cloves garlic, minced (about 1 tablespoon)

2 Anaheim chiles, stemmed, seeded, and cut into ½-inch-wide strips

1 large jalapeño chile, stemmed, seeded, and diced

2 Roma tomatoes, cored, seeded, and diced

Shredded beef from 1 recipe Uno-Dos-Tres Shredded Beef and Broth (page 156)

2 teaspoons kosher salt

2 teaspoons freshly ground black pepper

½ cup Tomatillo-Chipotle Salsa (page 142)

½ cup broth from Uno-Dos-Tres Shredded Beef and Broth (page 156)

¼ cup chopped fresh cilantro leaves

12 to 16 corn tortillas

FOR SERVING

Diced red onion or thinly sliced green onions, green parts only

Chopped fresh cilantro leaves

Shredded Monterey Jack or grated cotija cheese

Pico de Gallo (page 139)

Quick-cooked shredded beef is sautéed with salsa and vegetables to make a succulent taco filling (known as *machaca*) with many uses, including a brunch *platillo* (see Variation). Serve on lightly crisped corn tortillas with cheese, onion, and hot sauce. I like to top the tacos with chicharrón (see page 10) for extra crunch and flavor.

Press **Sauté—normal/medium** on the Instant Pot and heat 2 tablespoons of the oil. Add the onion, garlic, Anaheim chiles, jalapeño, and tomatoes. Cook, stirring occasionally, for about 3 minutes, until the vegetables are slightly softened. Add the shredded beef, salt, pepper, salsa, and broth. Cook, stirring occasionally, for 3 to 5 minutes, until the mixture is dry and thick. (It should not be saucy; if it is, using a slotted spoon, transfer the beef to a plate, then simmer the cooking liquid until very thick. Return the beef to the pot and stir to combine.) Stir in the cilantro. Press **Cancel**.

In a skillet over medium-high heat, warm the remaining 1 tablespoon oil. One at a time, add the tortillas and cook for 2 to 3 minutes per side, until crisped and spotty brown on both sides. Transfer to a large plate.

Transfer the machaca to a serving bowl. Serve with the diced onion, cilantro, Monterey Jack cheese, pico de gallo, and the tortillas for making tacos.

NOTE You may substitute store-bought jarred or fresh green salsa, ideally made with tomatillos, for the Tomatillo-Chipotle Salsa.

VARIATION

For a hearty machaca platillo, serve the machaca with Arroz Rojo (page 127), Refried Pinto Beans (page 124), and warmed flour tortillas.

CARNITAS

In Mexico, carnitas (literally, "little meats") simmer for hours in a large copper pot until the pork is fork-tender and falling off the bone. This version produces succulent meat in less than an hour. Enjoy as a traditional *platillo* with a tart tomatillo salsa, or in tacos, in burritos (see page 119), or to make my favorite tamale (see page 97).

Season the pork with the salt and pepper.

Press **Sauté—normal/medium** on the Instant Pot and heat the lard. Working in batches, add the pork in a single layer and cook for 3 to 5 minutes per side until well browned on all sides. Transfer to a large plate. Press **Cancel**. Add the onion, garlic, and water, then use a wooden spoon to scrape up any browned bits on the bottom of the pot. Return the pork and any accumulated juices to the pot.

Secure the lid and set the Pressure Release to **Sealing**. Press **Meat/Stew**, then set the cooking time for 30 minutes.

When the cooking program is complete, press **Cancel**. Let the pressure release naturally for 20 minutes, then move the Pressure Release to **Venting** to release any remaining steam. Open the pot and let cool for 10 minutes, then serve with the salsa, avocado, diced onion, cilantro, chicharrón (if using), and tortillas.

NOTE   Save any residual fat left in the Instant Pot to use in a skillet to crisp up and fry your carnitas or for use in other recipes, such as tamales or Chile Verde (page 75).

Serves 4 to 6

2½ pounds boneless pork shoulder, cut into 1½-inch pieces

1 teaspoon kosher salt

1 teaspoon freshly ground black pepper

1 tablespoon fresh lard (see page 10) or vegetable oil

½ white onion, thickly sliced

4 large garlic cloves, cut in half

1½ cups water

FOR SERVING

Fresh Tomatillo Salsa (page 143)

Warm corn tortillas

Diced avocado

Diced white onion

Chopped fresh cilantro leaves

Crumbled chicharrón (optional)

Warmed tortillas

CHILE VERDE

A celebration of all things chile, this is my take on the dish that has become a staple in the American Southwest. I think it tastes best when moderately spicy. In late summer, when Hatch chiles are in season, I'll use them instead of poblanos.

Line a cast-iron griddle or skillet with aluminum foil, set over high heat, and roast the tomatillos and serrano, turning often, for 5 to 7 minutes, until lightly charred and slightly softened. Transfer to a blender. Dice 1 Anaheim chile and 1 poblano chile and set aside. Add the remaining 2 Anaheims and 1 poblano to the blender and puree until smooth.

Press **Sauté—normal/medium** on the Instant Pot and heat the lard. Add half of the pork in a single layer and cook, stirring occasionally, for about 5 minutes, until lightly browned. Season with 1¼ teaspoons of the salt and ¾ teaspoon of the pepper, then, using a slotted spoon, transfer the pork to a plate. Add the remaining pork, the onion, garlic, and cumin and cook, stirring occasionally, for about 2 minutes, until lightly browned. Season with the remaining 1¼ teaspoons salt and the remaining ¾ teaspoon pepper. Add the flour and cook, stirring frequently, for about 2 minutes, until the flour begins to brown. Add the reserved pork, the broth, tomatoes, and potatoes (if using) and scrape up any browned bits on the bottom of the pot. Press **Cancel**.

Secure the lid and set the Pressure Release to **Sealing**. Press **Meat/Stew**, then set the cooking time for 25 minutes. When the cooking program is complete, press **Cancel**. Let the pressure release naturally for 20 minutes, then move the Pressure Release to **Venting** to release any remaining steam. Open the pot and stir in the reserved diced Anaheim and poblano chiles. Taste and adjust the seasoning with salt and pepper if needed. Serve with the rice, passing the sour cream, cilantro, diced onion, and avocado on the side.

Serves 4

3 tomatillos, husked

1 serrano chile, stemmed

3 Anaheim chiles, roasted (see page 6), seeded, and peeled

2 poblano chiles, roasted (see page 6), seeded, and peeled

2 tablespoons fresh lard (see page 10) or vegetable oil

2 pounds boneless pork shoulder, cut into ½-inch cubes

2½ teaspoons kosher salt

1½ teaspoons freshly ground black pepper

1 small white or yellow onion, diced

8 large garlic cloves, minced

1 tablespoon ground cumin

3 tablespoons all-purpose flour

2½ cups chicken broth

3 Roma tomatoes, cored and diced (about 2 cups), or one 14½-ounce can diced tomatoes, drained

8 ounces red or white potatoes, peeled and diced (optional)

FOR SERVING

Arroz Blanco (page 134)

Sour cream

Chopped fresh cilantro leaves

Diced red onion

Diced avocado

PORK ALBÓNDIGAS IN GREEN SAUCE WITH CHICHARRÓN

Serves 4

1 small white or yellow onion, roughly diced

4 large garlic cloves, peeled

1 serrano chile, stemmed

½ cup cooked white rice or fresh bread crumbs

1 large egg white

2 tablespoons chopped fresh cilantro leaves, flat-leaf parsley, or epazote

2 teaspoons kosher salt

1 teaspoon freshly ground black pepper

½ teaspoon dried Mexican oregano, rubbed between your fingers

¼ teaspoon aniseeds or cumin seeds

1¼ pounds ground pork

1 cup chicken broth or beef broth

2 tablespoons vegetable oil

1 cup Salsa Verde (page 140)

FOR SERVING
Crumbled chicharrón

Diced white onion

Chopped fresh cilantro leaves

Sour cream (optional)

Salsa Verde (page 140; optional)

Arroz Blanco (page 134)

The trick to handling delicate meatballs in the Instant Pot is to cook them first and brown them afterward, when they have firmed up. These tasty *albóndigas* are served in a rich, brothy salsa—perfect for soaking up with rice. Crunchy chicharrón (see page 10) is a delicious garnish.

In a food processor, combine the onion, garlic, serrano chile, and rice. Pulse until the mixture is very finely chopped. Transfer to a bowl and add the egg white, cilantro, salt, pepper, oregano, and aniseeds. Mix thoroughly, then crumble in the ground pork. Mix with your hands until the ingredients are evenly distributed. Divide the mixture into 16 equal portions and, with moistened hands, roll each into a ball.

Pour the broth into the Instant Pot and place a wire metal steam rack in the pot. Place the meatballs in a single layer on the rack.

Secure the lid and set the Pressure Release to **Sealing**. Press **Meat/Stew**, then set the cooking time for 10 minutes.

When the cooking program is complete, press **Cancel**. Perform a quick pressure release by moving the Pressure Release handle to **Venting**. Using tongs, transfer the meatballs to a plate and cover with aluminum foil to keep warm.

Wearing heat-resistant mitts, remove the steam rack, lift the inner pot out of the Instant Pot housing, and pour the cooking liquid into a small bowl; set aside. Wipe out the inner pot and return it to the housing.

CONTINUED

Press **Sauté—high** on the Instant Pot and heat the oil. Add the meatballs and cook, turning occasionally, for about 5 minutes, until lightly browned on all sides. Press **Cancel**. Using the tongs, return the meatballs to the plate. Wearing heat-resistant mitts, lift the inner pot out of the housing, then pour off and discard the oil. Return the inner pot to the housing, then press **Sauté—high**. Add the salsa and ½ cup of the reserved cooking liquid to the pot. Return the meatballs to the pot, placing them in a single layer. Bring to a simmer and cook for about 5 minutes, until heated through. Press **Cancel**.

Replace the lid without securing it and let stand for 5 minutes. If you would like the sauce a little thinner, stir in reserved cooking liquid until the sauce reaches the desired consistency. Taste and adjust the seasoning with salt and pepper if needed.

Divide the albóndigas and sauce among warmed bowls. Top with chicharrón, diced onion, and cilantro and serve with sour cream (if using), salsa verde (if using), and rice on the side.

NOTE   If you like, you can substitute ground turkey or chicken for the ground pork.

COCHINITA PIBIL

In the Yucatán region, pork is seasoned with earthy achiote, spices, citrus, and garlic; wrapped in banana leaves; and pit-roasted. Here, the chunks of pork are enclosed in foil packets, so the pork cooks in its delicious juices. Serve with Basic Black Beans (page 23) and any rice recipe in this book for a Yucatecan feast.

To marinate the pork: In a large bowl, combine the onion, garlic, serranos, achiote paste, vinegar, cumin, lime juice, salt, cilantro, and 1 tablespoon of the vegetable oil. Using a fork, mash the mixture to a paste. Add the pork pieces and stir until evenly coated. Cover and refrigerate for at least 1 hour but preferably overnight.

Press **Sauté—normal/medium** on the Instant Pot and heat the remaining 2 tablespoons oil. Working in batches, add the pork in a single layer and cook, stirring occasionally, for 3 to 5 minutes until the marinade is set. Transfer to a large plate. Press **Cancel**.

Cut four 10-inch squares of aluminum foil and lay them out on a work surface. Evenly divide the pork among the squares, followed by the onion rings, jalapeño rounds, and tomato slices. Fold the edges of the foil together to seal each packet.

Pour 1½ cups water into the Instant Pot, then place the long-handled wire rack in the pot. Arrange the packets on the rack, overlapping them to fit. Secure the lid and set the Pressure Release to **Sealing**. Press **Meat/Stew**, then set the cooking time for 35 minutes. When the cooking program is complete, press **Cancel**. Let the pressure release naturally for 20 minutes, then move the Pressure Release to **Venting** to release any remaining steam.

Open the pot. Wearing heat-resistant mitts, grasp the rack's handles and carefully lift the rack out of the pot. Using tongs, transfer the packets to individual plates and let cool for 5 minutes before serving. Let the diners open their own packet at the table and pass diced onion, avocado, cilantro, lime wedges, and tortillas on the side.

Serves 4 to 6

MARINATED PORK
½ small white or yellow onion, minced

4 large garlic cloves, minced

2 serrano chiles, stemmed and minced (with seeds)

3 tablespoons achiote paste (see page 9), crumbled

2 tablespoons white vinegar

1 tablespoon ground cumin

1 tablespoon fresh lime juice

1 tablespoon kosher salt

Leaves from ½ bunch cilantro, chopped

3 tablespoons vegetable oil

2½ pounds boneless pork shoulder, trimmed of fat and cut into 2-inch pieces

One ¼-inch-thick slice from 1 white or red onion, rings separated

1 jalapeño chile, stemmed and sliced into thin rounds (with seeds)

1 Roma tomato, sliced into thin rounds

FOR SERVING
Diced white onion

Diced avocado

Chopped fresh cilantro leaves

Lime wedges

Warmed corn tortillas

PORK BELLY WITH AGAVE-CHIPOTLE GLAZE

Serves 4

3 cups water

½ cup plus 1 teaspoon agave syrup

½ cup firmly packed crushed piloncillo (see page 12) or dark brown sugar

½ cup chiles de árbol, stemmed

2 dried chipotle chiles, stemmed, or 2 chipotle chiles in adobo sauce

1 habanero chile, cut in half (with seeds)

Three ½-inch-thick slices fresh ginger

2 garlic cloves, crushed and peeled

One ½-inch-thick slice from 1 white or yellow onion

¼ cup plus 2 tablespoons kosher salt

1 tablespoon black peppercorns

One 2-pound piece pork belly with rind, cut into several large pieces (to fit into inner pot)

1 tablespoon vegetable oil

1 cup chicken broth

1 cup dry white wine, such as Sauvignon Blanc

This is a two-day process of brining, cooking, refrigerating, and cooking some more. But if you love pork belly, it will be well worth the effort. The heat of the habanero, combined with the sweetness of agave and *piloncillo* is dynamite. It's delicious served in small crispy bites with Corn Esquites (page 105) or Nopales Salad (page 114).

In the Instant Pot, combine the water, the ½ cup agave syrup, the piloncillo, árbol chiles, chipotle chiles, habanero chile, ginger, garlic, onion, salt, and peppercorns. Press **Sauté—high** and bring to a boil. Cook, stirring to dissolve the sugar, for about 5 minutes, then press **Cancel**. Let the brine cool to room temperature.

Using a sharp knife, score the fat side of each piece of pork belly with 1-inch diamond shapes, cutting only about ¼ inch deep; do not cut into the meat. Place in a shallow glass or ceramic container just large enough to hold the pork belly in one layer and pour in the cooled brine. Place a piece of plastic wrap directly against the pork, then place a plate on top to weight it down so it's fully submerged. Refrigerate for at least 12 hours or up to 48 hours.

Remove the pork from the brine and pat dry with paper towels. Pour the brine through a wire-mesh strainer set over a bowl. Reserve the solids in the strainer and 1 cup of the brine.

Press **Sauté—high** on the Instant Pot and heat the oil. Add 1 piece of the pork, fat side down, and place a 7-inch cake pan and a few heavy cans on top. Cook for 5 to 7 minutes, until the pork is deeply browned. Remove the weights and cake pan and turn the pork. Replace the cake pan and weights and cook for 5 to 7 minutes, until the second side is deeply browned. Transfer to a plate and brown the remaining pieces of pork in the same way, then transfer to the plate. Press **Cancel**.

Wearing heat-resistant mitts, lift the inner pot out of the Instant Pot housing and pour off the fat. Return the inner pot to the housing. Add the reserved solids from the brine, the 1 cup reserved brine, the broth, and the wine. Return the pork to the pot, placing the pieces in a single layer. Place a couple of small heatproof plates on top to keep the pork fully submerged in the liquid.

Secure the lid and set the Pressure Release to **Sealing**. Press **Meat/Stew**, then set the cooking time for 35 minutes.

When the cooking program is complete, press **Cancel**. Let the pressure release naturally for 20 minutes, then move the Pressure Release to **Venting** to release any remaining steam. Open the pot and remove the plates. Using tongs, carefully transfer the pork to a shallow glass or ceramic container just large enough to hold the pork belly in one layer. Wearing heat-resistant mitts, lift the inner pot out of the Instant Pot housing and pour the cooking liquid through a wire-mesh strainer set over a bowl. Discard the solids in the strainer, then pour the liquid over the pork. Place a piece of plastic wrap directly against the pork, then place a plate on top to weight it down so it's fully submerged. Refrigerate for a minimum of 6 hours.

Remove the pork from the liquid and pat dry with paper towels; reserve the liquid. Cut the pork into about 2-inch squares.

Heat a large nonstick skillet over medium heat. Working in batches, add the pork belly pieces fat side down and cook for 5 to 7 minutes, until crisp. As each batch is ready, using the tongs, transfer to a large plate. When all of the pieces are crisped, again using the tongs, return them crisped side up to the pan, then add 1½ cups of the reserved liquid and the remaining 1 teaspoon agave syrup. Bring to a simmer and cook for 3 to 5 minutes, until the liquid is reduced to a thick glaze and the pork is heated through. Serve hot, with the glaze spooned over the pork.

NOTE   For a spicier finish, add ½ habanero chile to the pan along with the cooking liquid and agave syrup.

CHORIZO, BLACK BEAN, AND SWEET POTATO TACOS

Serves 4 to 6

1 pound orange-flesh sweet potatoes, peeled and cut into 1-inch chunks (about 3 cups)

1 cup water

1½ teaspoons kosher salt

2 tablespoons vegetable oil

1 large white or yellow onion, diced

3 garlic cloves, minced

1 poblano chile or green bell pepper, stemmed, seeded, and diced

1 teaspoon freshly ground black pepper

1 teaspoon ground cumin

1 teaspoon dried Mexican oregano

8 ounces Mexican-style chorizo sausage, casing removed

1½ cups drained Basic Black Beans (page 23)

FOR SERVING
Avocado slices or Avocado-Tomatillo Sauce (page 150)

Chipotle and Garlic Salsa (page 153)

Habanero Hot Sauce (page 144)

Pico de Gallo (page 139)

Grated cotija cheese

Diced white onion

Chopped fresh cilantro

Warmed corn tortillas

This dish cooks in less than 30 minutes in the Instant Pot, which makes it very doable for a weeknight dinner. If you have a Mexican market nearby that makes its own chorizo, you're in luck, but any high-quality store-bought Mexican chorizo will do.

In the Instant Pot, combine the sweet potatoes, water, and ½ teaspoon of the salt. Secure the lid and set the Pressure Release to **Sealing**. Press **Pressure Cook**, then set the cooking time for 2 minutes.

When the cooking program is complete, press **Cancel**. Perform a quick pressure release by moving the Pressure Release to **Venting**. Open the pot, then, wearing heat-resistant mitts, lift the inner pot out of the Instant Pot housing and drain the sweet potatoes in a colander.

Rinse the inner pot, wipe it dry, and return it to the housing. Press **Sauté—high** and heat the oil. Add the onion, garlic, and poblano chile and cook, stirring occasionally, for about 2 minutes, until the vegetables just begin to soften. Add the remaining 1 teaspoon salt, the pepper, cumin, and oregano and cook, stirring, for about 1 minute. Transfer the mixture to a plate and set aside.

Add the chorizo to the pot and cook, stirring occasionally and breaking up the sausage into bite-size bits, for about 10 minutes, until well cooked. Add the black beans and onion mixture and cook, stirring occasionally, for about 2 minutes, until hot. Stir in the sweet potatoes, replace the lid without securing it, and press **Cancel**. Let stand for 5 minutes, until the potatoes are heated through. Taste and adjust the seasoning with salt and pepper if needed.

Transfer to a bowl and serve with the avocado, salsa, habanero sauce, pico de gallo, cotija, diced onion, cilantro, and tortillas for making tacos.

TACOS AL PASTOR

Al pastor is the iconic Mexico City taco: a stack of seasoned pork cooked on a rotating spit and then sliced and crisped to order. This adaptation, made with diced pork, produces a very creditable *al pastor*. The finishing touch of pineapple is traditional, and very good.

In the Instant Pot, combine the pork, ½ teaspoon of the salt, and the water. Secure the lid and set the Pressure Release to **Sealing**. Press **Meat/Stew**, then set the cooking time for 30 minutes.

Meanwhile, in a bowl, stir together the ground chile, achiote paste, garlic salt, cumin, pepper, garlic, oil, and vinegar. Stir in the pineapple and onion.

In a large skillet over medium heat, cooking the pineapple mixture, stirring frequently, for about 5 minutes, until soft. Remove from the heat.

When the cooking program is complete, press **Cancel**. Perform a quick pressure release by moving the Pressure Release to **Venting**. Open the pot and let rest for 10 minutes.

Using a slotted spoon, transfer the pork to the skillet with the pineapple mixture, then add ½ cup of the cooking liquid. Cook over medium-high heat, stirring gently, for about 5 minutes, until the mixture looks dry and the pork is slightly crusted.

Transfer to a bowl and serve with the avocado, diced onion, cilantro, and tortillas for making tacos.

Serves 4 to 6

2 pounds boneless pork shoulder, cut into 1-inch pieces

1½ teaspoons kosher salt

¾ cup water

¼ cup California or guajillo chile powder

1 tablespoon achiote paste (see page 9)

2 teaspoons garlic salt

2 teaspoons ground cumin

1 teaspoon freshly ground black pepper

6 garlic cloves, chopped (about 2 tablespoons)

3 tablespoons vegetable oil

3 tablespoons white vinegar

⅓ cup finely diced fresh pineapple or drained canned pineapple chunks

½ white onion, diced

FOR SERVING

Diced avocado or Avocado-Tomatillo Sauce (page 150)

Diced white or red onion

Chopped fresh cilantro leaves

Warmed corn tortillas

OAXACAN CHILEAJO

Serves 4 to 6

4 pounds bone-in pork shoulder, meat cut from the bone (you should have about 3 pounds of meat and 1 pound of bone)

3 cups water

1 teaspoon kosher salt

8 black peppercorns

8 chiles de árbol

4 large or 6 medium guajillo chiles, stemmed and seeded

1 ancho chile, stemmed and seeded

2 cups boiling water

5 large garlic cloves, unpeeled

½ small white or yellow onion, roughly diced

½ teaspoon ground cumin

½ teaspoon dried Mexican oregano

1 whole clove

1 Roma tomato, cored

6 tomatillos, husked and roughly chopped

2 tablespoons fresh lard (see page 10) or vegetable oil

FOR SERVING

Diced white onion

Chopped fresh cilantro leaves

Arroz Blanco (page 134)

Warmed corn tortillas

There are a number of steps here, such as frying the chile puree, but each one builds flavor. To save time, some of these steps are completed on the stove top. Be sure to read the entire recipe through before beginning. The meat is cooked with the bone to add flavor and body to the simple red mole sauce.

———————

Cut the pork into 1½-inch pieces and place in the Instant Pot, along with the bone. Add the water, salt, and peppercorns.

Secure the lid and set the Pressure Release to **Sealing**. Press **Meat/Stew**, then set the cooking time for 20 minutes.

While the pork is cooking, in a large skillet over medium-high heat, toast the árbol, guajillo, and ancho chiles, turning them occasionally, for about 1 minute; be careful not to burn them. Transfer to a plate and let cool. Remove and discard all the seeds and ribs from the chiles, then tear the chiles into small pieces and add to a heatproof bowl. Pour in the boiling water and let stand for 10 minutes, until softened. Drain the chiles, discarding the soaking liquid, then place in a blender.

In the same skillet, toast the garlic cloves over medium heat, turning occasionally, for about 5 minutes, until spotty brown on all sides. Transfer to a plate. Let cool, then peel the cloves and add them to the blender along with the onion, cumin, oregano, and clove. Set aside.

When the cooking program is complete, press **Cancel**. Perform a quick pressure release by moving the Pressure Release to **Venting**. Open the pot and add 1 cup of the cooking liquid to the ingredients in the blender. Blend until very smooth, scraping down the blender as needed.

Using a slotted spoon, transfer the meat to a plate. Remove and discard the bone. Add the tomato and tomatillos to the cooking liquid in the pot. Press **Sauté—high**, bring to a simmer, and cook for about 5 minutes, until the vegetables have softened. Press **Cancel**. Using the slotted spoon, transfer the vegetables to a small bowl. Reserve the cooking liquid.

In a Dutch oven over medium heat, warm the lard. Add the meat and cook, stirring gently so as not to break it up, for 3 to 5 minutes, until lightly browned. Pour in the chile puree; do not rinse the blender. Cook, stirring so the chile puree doesn't stick to the pot, for about 5 minutes, until thickened and darkened.

Add the tomato and tomatillos to the now-empty blender and blend until smooth. Pour the puree into the pot with the pork and cook, stirring occasionally, for about 5 minutes, until thickened.

Meanwhile, wearing heat-resistant mitts, lift the inner pot out of the Instant Pot housing and pour the remaining cooking liquid into the blender. Swish it around to loosen any residual puree, then pour into the pot with the pork. Bring to a simmer and cook uncovered, stirring occasionally, for about 30 minutes, until thickened. Taste and adjust the seasoning with salt and pepper if needed. Serve, passing diced onion, cilantro, rice, and tortillas on the side.

BEER-BRAISED CHIPOTLE BEEF WITH VEGETABLES

Serves 4 to 6

2 Roma tomatoes, cored and roughly chopped

1 tomatillo, husked and roughly chopped

3 garlic cloves, peeled

2 chipotle chiles in adobo sauce

2 slices bacon, cut into 1-inch pieces

1 small white or yellow onion, thinly sliced

1 tablespoon fresh lard (see page 10) or vegetable oil

2½ pounds boneless beef chuck roast, trimmed of fat and cut into 2-inch cubes

2 teaspoons kosher salt

1 teaspoon freshly ground black pepper

½ teaspoon dried Mexican oregano

6 fresh epazote leaves, shredded, or ¼ cup fresh cilantro leaves, chopped

¾ cup dark beer, such as Negra Modelo

¾ cup beef broth

1½ pounds potatoes, sweet potatoes, brussels sprouts, and/or carrots, cut into 2-inch pieces

Any stew with beef, beer, chiles, and bacon is bound to be a hit. Here, chipotles in adobo lend their smoky heat to a stew chock-full of seasonal vegetables. The fresh epazote (see page 12) adds an authentic Mexican flavor. The recipe uses only half a can of beer, so you'll just have to drink the other half.

In a blender, combine the tomatoes, tomatillo, garlic, and chipotles. Blend until smooth, scraping down the blender as needed. Set aside.

Press **Sauté—high** on the Instant Pot and add the bacon. Cook, stirring occasionally, for 3 to 5 minutes, until the fat is rendered. Add the onion and cook, stirring occasionally, for about 5 minutes, until the onion is translucent. Transfer the bacon-onion mixture to a small plate.

Add the lard to the Instant Pot. Working in batches, add the beef in a single layer and cook until well browned on all sides, about 2 minutes per side. Transfer to a large plate. When all the beef has been browned, season with the salt, pepper, and oregano. Press **Cancel**. Wearing heat-resistant mitts, lift out the inner pot from the Instant Pot housing, then pour off and discard the fat. Return the inner pot to the housing.

Press **Sauté—normal/medium** on the Instant Pot. Pour in the tomato-chipotle puree and cook, stirring occasionally and scraping up any browned bits on the bottom of the pot, for about 3 minutes, until thickened. Return the bacon-onion mixture and the beef to the pot. Add the epazote, beer, and broth and stir to combine.

CONTINUED

FOR SERVING

Pico de Gallo (page 139)

Grated cotija cheese

Diced red onion or thinly sliced green onions, green parts only

Diced avocado

Chopped fresh cilantro

Warmed tortillas

Secure the lid and set the Pressure Release to **Sealing**. Press **Meat/Stew**, then set the cooking time for 25 minutes.

When the cooking program is complete, press **Cancel**. Perform a quick pressure release by moving the Pressure Release to **Venting**. Open the pot, then use a slotted spoon to transfer the beef to a bowl. Cover with aluminum foil to keep warm. Using a spoon, skim off and discard the fat on the surface of the cooking liquid.

Press **Sauté—high** on the Instant Pot. Add the vegetables and cook, stirring occasionally, for about 15 minutes, until a knife inserted into the vegetables meets no resistance and the cooking liquid is slightly thickened.

Return the meat and any accumulated juices to the pot and stir to combine. Cook for about 1 minute, then press **Cancel**. Taste and adjust the seasoning with salt and pepper if needed. Serve the stew with the pico de gallo, cotija cheese, diced onion, avocado, cilantro, and tortillas on the side.

NOTES Corn is a good addition to the stew. Shuck 1 ear, cut it into 4 pieces, and add it along with the other vegetables

If you prefer the cooking liquid a little thicker, in a small bowl, stir together 1 tablespoon cornstarch and 2 tablespoons water or beer, then stir the mixture into the cooking liquid when the vegetables are almost done. Bring to a simmer and cook, stirring constantly, for about 2 minutes, until the liquid is fully thickened.

For a spicier stew, stir in minced chipotle chiles in adobo sauce just before serving.

BEEF AND GREEN CHILE STEW WITH POTATOES

A meal in a bowl, this is northern Mexican home cooking at its best, with a gentle heat that's quite addictive. The beef emerges from the Instant Pot juicy and tender in just 25 minutes, about one-third of the time it would take to simmer on the stove top. Charring the chiles is not an essential step, but it adds a wonderful smoky flavor to the *guisado*. In season, fresh Hatch chiles are an excellent substitute for the more common poblanos.

Press **Sauté—high** on the Instant Pot and heat the oil. Working in batches, add the beef in a single layer and cook until well browned on all sides, about 2 minutes per side. Season the beef with salt as it cooks, then transfer to a large plate .Add the onion, garlic, one-third of the poblano chiles, the jalapeño, and the tomatoes. Cook, stirring occasionally and scraping up any browned bits on the bottom of the pot, for about 5 minutes, until the onion is softened. Stir in the cumin, oregano, pepper, and bay and cook, stirring, for about 1 minute. Return the beef to the pot, add the potatoes and broth, and stir to combine. Press **Cancel**.

Secure the lid and set the Pressure Release to **Sealing**. Press **Pressure Cook**, then set the cooking time for 25 minutes.

When the cooking program is complete, press **Cancel**. Perform a quick pressure release by moving the Pressure Release to **Venting**. Open the pot, then stir in the remaining poblano chiles. Taste and adjust the seasoning with salt and pepper if needed. Serve the stew topped with sour cream and green onions, with tortillas on the side.

NOTES   For a milder stew, substitute Anaheim chiles for the poblanos and omit the jalapeño. For a spicier version, add 1 or 2 more jalapeños.

Serves 4

2 tablespoons vegetable oil or fresh lard (see page 10)

2½ pounds boneless beef chuck roast, trimmed of fat and cut into 1-inch pieces

2 teaspoons kosher salt

1 large white or yellow onion, cut into 1-inch dice

3 large garlic cloves, minced

3 poblano chiles, roasted (see page 6), seeded, peeled, and cut into 1-inch pieces

1 jalapeño chile, stemmed, seeded, and minced

2 large Roma tomatoes, cored, seeded, and diced, or one 14½-ounce can diced fire-roasted tomatoes, drained

2 teaspoons ground cumin

1 teaspoon dried Mexican oregano

1 teaspoon freshly ground black pepper

1 bay leaf

12 ounces red potatoes, cut into 1-inch chunks

1¼ cups beef broth

Sour cream for serving

Thinly sliced green onions, green parts only, or diced white onion for serving

Warmed tortillas for serving

TAMALES

Those of us who love tamales really don't love the busywork of tending the steamer while they cook or waiting impatiently for a couple of hours. This quick recipe delivers perfectly cooked tamales in less than an hour, and you don't have to worry about adding water as they cook.

Tamales are well worth the fuss and time spent on them. I prefer to use a dry masa harina, such as Maseca brand, for them. Most prepared tamale masas sold in Mexican groceries are already seasoned, and I like to do that myself.

The masa should be seasoned with salt until it tastes good—don't be afraid to taste a bit. It should be fluffy and rather wet—almost the consistency of cake frosting. Make sure the shortening, pork lard, and broth are well chilled. And most important, be sure the filling is juicy and flavorful, but not dripping wet, which would prevent the masa from setting.

Tamales can be filled with almost anything you like and any combination of flavors you like. A few of the more traditional fillings are given here, but once you have made tamales a few times and are comfortable with the technique, don't be afraid to stray a bit and create your own unique combos!

Tamales may be wrapped in dried corn husks or in banana (also called plantain) leaves. The banana leaf adds subtle flavor and looks quite dramatic due to its size and color. Both types of leaves are available at well-stocked Mexican groceries. Banana leaves may also be found at Asian groceries.

The tamales will seem a bit soft when they come out of the Instant Pot, but don't worry, as they firm up nicely. Next-day tamales (unlikely, but possible) will be a little dry, so offer more salsa when serving.

BASIC TAMALES

Makes about 2 dozen
5-inch tamales

3 cups Maseca brand
masa harina

2 teaspoons baking powder

1½ teaspoons kosher salt

2 cups warm water, plus more
as needed

¾ cup vegetable shortening,
chilled

½ cup fresh lard
(see page 10), chilled

1 cup chicken broth, chilled,
store-bought or homemade

36 large corn husks, soaked
and drained (see How to
Prepare Corn Husks,
page 97), or about thirty
10-inch banana leaf squares
(see How to Prepare Banana
Leaves, page 97)

2 cups filling of your choice,
plus salsa for serving (see
Traditional Fillings for
Tamales, page 97, for ideas)

Garnishes of your choice (see
On the Table, page 119) for
serving

1   In a large bowl, whisk together the masa harina, baking powder, and salt.
Add the water and, using a wooden spoon or your hand, mix until a dough
forms. The dough should be soft and pliable but not wet; if it is too dry, mix in
additional water 1 tablespoon at a time until it reaches the proper consistency.

2   In the bowl of a stand mixer fitted with the paddle attachment or in a large
bowl and using a handheld mixer, beat the shortening and lard on medium
speed for about 5 minutes, until fluffy and light. With the mixer running on
low speed, add the dough about ¼ cup at a time, beating thoroughly after each
addition and alternating with about ¼ cup of the broth; scrape down the bowl
as needed. After all the dough and broth have been added, continue to beat
the mixture on medium speed for about 1 minute, until perfectly smooth. Taste
a small amount for salt; it should be flavorful but not salty. Beat in additional
salt if needed.

3   If using corn husks: Lay a lightly moistened kitchen towel on your work surface.
Place a corn husk on the towel with the narrow end facing away from you (use
the largest husks first, but smaller ones can be overlapped as needed). Using a
teaspoon, spread about ¼ cup of the masa over the center of the husk, leaving
a 2-inch margin at the top and bottom and a 1-inch margin on each side. Place
2 tablespoons filling down the center. Fold in the sides of the husk to overlap
the filling, then fold up the bottom, but not too tightly; you can fold down
the top or leave it open. Tie loosely with a strip of corn husk. Form additional
tamales in the same way until you have used up all of the masa and/or filling.

4   If using banana leaves: Lay a lightly moistened kitchen towel on your work
surface, then place a banana leaf square on the towel. Using a teaspoon,
spread about ⅓ cup of the masa over the center of the leaf, leaving a 2-inch
margin on all sides. Place 2 tablespoons filling down the center. Fold the two
sides in first over the filling. It should be about 1 inch thick when folded.

Then fold up the top and bottom to make a rectangular shape. Tie with a strip of banana leaf.

5   Pour 1½ cups water into the Instant Pot and place the long-handled wire rack in the pot. Place a single layer of corn husks or banana leaf on the rack. Place the tamales on the rack, standing them on end, with the open ends facing up if the tamales were folded only on three sides. (You may need to cook in two batches if your tamales are plump.) They should be snug but not tightly packed. A few tamales can be laid flat on the top, but be careful not to block the vent or float valve on the lid.

6   Secure the lid and set the Pressure Release to **Sealing**. Press **Pressure Cook**, then set the cooking time for 45 minutes.

7   When the cooking program is complete, press **Cancel**. Perform a quick pressure release by moving the Pressure Release to **Venting**. Open the pot, and, using tongs, remove a tamale from the center of the pot. Carefully open the tamale—the masa will be very soft, but if the husk peels away easily, the tamales are ready. If not, return the tester tamale to the pot, secure the lid once again, then set the Pressure Release to **Sealing**. Press **Pressure Cook**, then set the cooking time for 10 minutes. When the cooking program is complete, press **Cancel**. Perform a quick pressure release by moving the Pressure Release to **Venting**. Open the pot and let stand for 10 minutes, loosely covered with the lid.

8   Using tongs, remove as many tamales as you need for serving. To keep the rest warm, replace the lid but do not secure it. Serve the tamales warm with the garnishes of your choice and salsa (to match the filling) on the side.

SPICY BLACK BEAN TAMALES

Makes about twenty-five 5-inch tamales

FILLING

3 cups drained Basic Black Beans (page 23), plus 1 cup of their cooking liquid

2 tablespoons vegetable oil

¼ white onion, minced

3 garlic cloves, minced

10 fresh epazote leaves, chopped, or ¼ teaspoon dried Mexican oregano

½ teaspoon red pepper flakes, or 1 chipotle chile in adobo sauce, minced

Leaves from ½ bunch cilantro, chopped

½ teaspoon kosher salt, or to taste

MASA

2 cups Maseca brand masa harina

1 teaspoon baking powder

1 teaspoon kosher salt

1⅓ cups Red Chile Salsa (page 141)

¾ cup vegetable shortening, chilled

1 cup cold water, or vegetable broth, chilled

36 large corn husks, soaked and drained (see facing page for directions on preparing), or about thirty 10-inch banana leaf squares (see facing page)

Garnishes of your choice (see On the Table, page 119)

To make the filling: In a blender, combine the black beans and their liquid, and puree until smooth.

Press **Sauté—normal/medium** on the Instant Pot and heat the oil. Add the onion, garlic, epazote, and red pepper flakes and cook, stirring occasionally, for about 5 minutes, until the onion is translucent. Add the pureed beans and the cilantro and cook, stirring occasionally, for about 20 minutes, until very thick; when the mixture starts to thicken, stir more frequently and scrape along the bottom of the pot. Press **Cancel**. Taste and adjust the seasoning with salt if needed; the mixture should be well seasoned. Transfer to a bowl and set aside.

To make the masa: In a bowl, whisk together the masa harina, baking powder, and salt. Add the salsa and, using a wooden spoon or your hand, mix until a dough forms. The dough should be soft and pliable but not wet; if it is too dry, mix in additional water 1 tablespoon at a time until it reaches the proper consistency.

See step 2 of Basic Tamales (page 94) for instructions on how to form the masa in a stand mixer or with a household mixer, using the chilled shortening and water.

If using corn husks, see step 3 of Basic Tamales for instructions on how to form the tamales.

If using banana leaves, see step 4 of Basic Tamales for instructions on how to form the tamales.

Cook the tamales according to the instructions in the Basic Tamales recipe, steps 5 through 7, reducing the **Pressure Cook** time to 40 minutes.

Serve the tamales warm with the garnishes of your choice.

TRADITIONAL FILLINGS
FOR TAMALES

Keep in mind that tamales fillings should be flavorful and moist but not drippy.
Don't be shy about adding salt and pepper—the filling should be well seasoned.
Each of the following makes about 2 cups, enough for a batch of Basic Tamales
(page 94).

- **Beef Filling:** In a skillet over medium-high heat, cook 2 cups shredded beef from Uno-Dos-Tres Shredded Beef and Broth (page 156) and ¾ cup Red Chile Salsa (page 141) until most of the moisture has evaporated but the mixture is still moist. Season to taste. Have additional red chile salsa for serving with the tamales.

- **Chicken Filling:** In a skillet over medium-high heat, cook 2 cups shredded chicken from Uno-Dos-Tres Shredded Chicken and Broth (page 154) and ¾ cup Salsa Verde (page 140) until most of the moisture has evaporated but the mixture is still moist. Season to taste. Have additional salsa verde for serving with the tamales.

- **Carnitas:** In a skillet over medium-high heat, cook 2 cups Carnitas (page 73) and ¾ cup Salsa Verde (page 140) until most of the moisture has evaporated but the mixture is still moist. Season to taste. Have additional salsa verde for serving with the tamales.

- **Corn, Chile, and Cheese Filling:** In a bowl, stir together 1 cup corn kernels cut from 2 medium ears grilled corn; 1 cup shredded Oaxacan cheese; and 3 poblano chiles, roasted (see page 6), seeded, peeled, and torn into strips. Season to taste. Have Salsa Verde (page 140) and Habanero Hot Sauce (page 144) for serving with the tamales.

HOW TO PREPARE DRIED CORN HUSKS

Separate the husks and soak in hot tap water until softened. Drain. Make ties by tearing long strips about ½ inch wide from the sides of longer husks, or tie the ends of two shorter strips together to make a long one.

HOW TO PREPARE BANANA LEAVES

If the leaves are frozen, thaw at room temperature before use. Using kitchen scissors, cut away and discard any hard, stringy ribs along edges or down the center of the leaf. Wipe the leaves with paper towels, then tear them into 10-inch squares. Soften the squares by quickly passing both sides of each one over a lit gas burner or by briefly pressing each side against the surface of a large skillet over high heat. Stack the softened leaves until ready to use.

chapter 4

VEGETARIAN

GREEN CHILE MAC 'N' CHEESE

Serves 4 to 6

2 tablespoons butter

1 small white onion, diced

6 garlic cloves, minced
(2 tablespoons)

1 jalapeño chile, stemmed
and minced (with seeds)

2 cups vegetable broth or
chicken broth

2 cups heavy cream

5 teaspoons kosher salt

1 tablespoon freshly ground
black pepper

1 pound large elbow
macaroni

½ cup Mexican crema or
sour cream

2 cups shredded mild
Cheddar cheese

1 cup shredded Monterey Jack
or pepper Jack cheese

2 poblano chiles, roasted
(see page 6), seeded, peeled,
and cut into 1-inch dice

Thinly sliced green onions,
green parts only, or chopped
fresh cilantro leaves for
serving

Pasta cooks perfectly in the Instant Pot, from start to finish. You'll find this Southwest-style mac and cheese rich, creamy, and cheesy, but definitely not bland. And it cooks up in about 15 minutes. Add more jalapeños for more kick, or use green Anaheim chiles for a milder dish.

Press **Sauté—normal/medium** on the Instant Pot and melt the butter. Add the onion, garlic, and jalapeño and cook, stirring occasionally, for about 3 minutes, until softened but not browned. Press **Cancel**. Add the broth, cream, salt, pepper, and macaroni, then stir to combine.

Secure the lid and set the Pressure Release to **Sealing**. Press **Pressure Cook**, then set the cooking time for 8 minutes.

When the cooking program is complete, press **Cancel**. Perform a quick pressure release by moving the Pressure Release to **Venting**. Open the pot, then add the crema, Cheddar cheese, and Jack cheese and stir until the cheeses have melted. Stir in the poblano chiles, then replace the lid without securing it. Let stand for 2 minutes. Taste and adjust the seasoning with salt and pepper if needed.

Serve the mac 'n' cheese right away, sprinkled with the green onions.

NOTES Serve the mac 'n' cheese topped with a sprinkle of crushed corn chips or with 6 ounces Mexican-style chorizo sausage, casing removed, cooked in a skillet, then crumbled.

For even more salty-cheesy flavor, add ½ cup grated cotija cheese.

VARIATION

For Chipotle Mac 'n' Cheese, substitute ¼ cup finely chopped chipotle chiles in adobo sauce for the poblano chiles.

TEXAS QUESO FUNDIDO

I'd never dream of messing with a Texas staple, so here are two versions of *queso*, one made with shredded Cheddar and Jack cheeses and one made with American cheese (see Variations). *Fundido* means "melted," and that's what this is: gooey and hot, to scoop up with chips or tortillas. My tasters liked both versions equally.

Press **Sauté—normal/medium** on the Instant Pot and heat the oil. Add the onion, garlic, serrano chiles, cumin, and pepper and cook, stirring constantly, for about 1 minute, until slightly softened. Add the broth and flour and stir until well combined. Press **Cancel**. Add the cream cheese, Cheddar cheese, Jack cheese, and tomato and stir until the cheeses melt.

Secure the lid and set the Pressure Release to **Sealing**. Press **Pressure Cook**, then set the cooking time for 1 minute.

When the cooking program is complete, press **Cancel**. Perform a quick pressure release by moving the Pressure Release to **Venting**. Open the pot, then whisk the queso until smooth. Press **Warm** and serve directly from the Instant Pot, or transfer to a warmed serving bowl. Serve with tostadas and flour tortillas for dipping.

CONTINUED

Serves 4 to 6

2 tablespoons vegetable oil

½ small white onion, minced, or 4 green onions, minced

2 large cloves garlic, minced

2 serrano chiles, stemmed and minced (with seeds)

1 teaspoon ground cumin

1 teaspoon freshly ground black pepper

1 cup vegetable broth or chicken broth

1 tablespoon all-purpose flour

½ cup cream cheese, cut into cubes

2 cups packed shredded mild yellow Cheddar cheese

1 cup packed shredded Monterey Jack cheese

1 large Roma tomato, cored, seeded, and diced

Tostadas or tortilla chips for serving

Warmed flour tortillas for serving

VARIATIONS

For Texas Queso Fundido with American cheese, reduce the broth to ½ cup, omit the flour, and substitute one 1-pound block processed American cheese, cut into ½-inch cubes, for the Cheddar and Monterey Jack cheeses.

For Queso Fundido con Chorizo, cook 6 ounces Mexican-style chorizo sausage, casing removed, in a skillet over medium heat until browned, about 5 minutes. Just before serving, crumble the cooked chorizo over the queso and sprinkle with 1 green onion, green part only, thinly sliced.

For Nachos, pile tortilla chips onto a heatproof platter. Top with spoonfuls of queso fundido, diced tomatoes, sliced pickled jalapeños (page 149), and anything else you like—cooked, crumbled chorizo, shredded pork, diced white onion, and chopped fresh cilantro leaves. Finish with more queso fundido and heat briefly under the broiler.

CORN ESQUITES

Making this classic Mexican street food—cooked corn with butter and chiles—is a snap with the Instant Pot. The quick cooking keeps kernels bursting with sweet flavor. Half the fun of *esquites* is loading on the salsas and cheese, so don't hold back. *Esquites* is a great side dish. I also like to spoon it onto tacos or guacamole.

In the Instant Pot, combine the corn, broth, wine, butter, and salt. Secure the lid and set the Pressure Release to **Sealing**. Press **Pressure Cook**, then set the cooking time for 4 minutes.

When the cooking program is complete, press **Cancel**. Perform a quick pressure release by moving the Pressure Release to **Venting**. Open the pot, then press **Sauté—normal/medium**. Cook, stirring occasionally, for 5 to 7 minutes, until most of the moisture has evaporated. Press **Cancel**.

Stir in the chipotle sauce, lime juice, and ¼ cup of the cotija. Taste and adjust the seasoning with salt if needed. Transfer to a serving bowl and sprinkle with the remaining cotija, the green onion, and ground chile. Serve the lime wedges on the side.

Serves 4

3½ cups fresh corn kernels (cut from 4 ears) or thawed frozen corn kernels

½ cup vegetable broth or chicken broth

½ cup white wine

4 tablespoons butter

¼ teaspoon kosher salt

2 tablespoons Chipotle and Garlic Salsa (page 153)

1 tablespoon fresh lime juice, plus lime wedges for serving

⅓ cup grated cotija cheese

1 green onion, green part only, thinly sliced

½ teaspoon guajillo or chipotle chile powder

RICE-STUFFED CHILES IN SPICY TOMATO SAUCE

Serves 4

STUFFED CHILES
8 poblano chiles

2 cups shredded Monterey Jack cheese

1 cup shredded mild yellow Cheddar cheese

3 cups cooked rice, such as Arroz Verde (page 131) (made with vegetable broth, if desired)

Leaves from ½ bunch cilantro, chopped

SPICY TOMATO SAUCE
4 Roma tomatoes, cored and cut into quarters

4 tomatillos, husked and roughly chopped

¼ cup diced white onion

2 large garlic cloves, sliced

½ cup water

1½ teaspoons kosher salt

¼ teaspoon dried Mexican oregano

3 chipotle chiles in adobo sauce

1 tablespoon olive oil

4 tablespoons butter

2 tablespoons chopped fresh cilantro leaves

The moderate chile heat in this vegetarian entrée is balanced by the rice, cheese, and lots of cilantro. You may substitute milder Anaheim chiles for some or all of the poblanos, and tone down the sauce with fewer chipotles. The spicy tomato sauce, called *salsa diabla*, is terrific with roasted or grilled vegetables, too. This is a quick recipe, but you'll need 3 cups of cooked rice at the ready.

To prepare the stuffed chiles: Lightly char the poblano chiles all over, being careful not to overcook, as they are easier to handle when half-cooked. (See roasting instructions on page 6.) Wrap the charred chiles in paper towels and let stand until cool enough to handle. Leaving on the stems for presentation, peel off the skins. Using a paring knife, slit open each chile on one side, from the stem to tip. Carefully pull out and discard the seeds.

In a bowl, toss together the Jack and Cheddar cheeses. Transfer 2 cups of the cheese mixture to another bowl, then stir in the rice and cilantro. Reserve the remaining 1 cup cheese mixture for sprinkling.

Using a teaspoon, stuff the chiles with the rice mixture, firmly packing in the filling. (The stuffed chiles may be placed in an airtight container and refrigerated for up to 1 day.)

Preheat the oven to 350°F.

To make the sauce: In the Instant Pot, combine the tomatoes, tomatillos, onion, garlic, water, salt, and oregano . Secure the lid and set the Pressure Release to **Sealing**. Press **Pressure Cook**, then set the cooking time for 2 minutes.

CONTINUED

When the cooking program is complete, press **Cancel**. Perform a quick pressure release by moving the Pressure Release handle to **Venting**. Open the pot, then, wearing heat-resistant mitts, lift the inner pot out of the Instant Pot housing. Set a wire-mesh strainer over a bowl and pour the contents of the pot into the strainer. Transfer the solids in the strainer to a blender, then pour in ½ cup of the strained liquid; discard the remainder. Add the chipotle chiles to the blender and puree until smooth, scraping down the blender as needed.

Rinse the inner pot, wipe it dry, and return it to the Instant Pot housing. Press **Sauté—normal/medium**, then add the oil and the tomato-chipotle puree. Cook, stirring occasionally, for 5 to 7 minutes, until thickened. Press **Cancel**, then stir in the butter and cilantro. Taste and adjust the seasoning with salt if needed.

Pour the sauce into a 9 by 13-inch baking dish and place the chiles, seam side up, on top in a single layer. Scatter the reserved cheese mixture on top and bake for about 5 minutes, until the cheese is melted and bubbling.

Serve right away.

VARIATIONS

For Chicken-and-Rice-Stuffed Chiles in Spicy Tomato Sauce, reduce the rice to 1 cup and add 2 cups shredded chicken from Uno-Dos-Tres Shredded Chicken and Broth (page 154).

For Rice-Stuffed Chiles in Salsa Verde, substitute 1½ cups Salsa Verde (page 140) for the Spicy Tomato Sauce and drizzle with sour cream after baking.

PAPAS CON CREMA Y CHILES

The distinctive flavor of roasted poblano chile *rajas* (strips) combined with cream complements the buttery little potatoes. This makes a great side dish for a special occasion, or use it to dress up a simple roast chicken or roasted vegetables. The Instant Pot does triple duty here: After the potatoes cook in the pot, the ingredients for a creamy sauce are sautéed, reduced, and pureed, Then it all comes together for a quick simmer.

In the Instant Pot, combine the potatoes, broth, wine, and salt. Secure the lid and set the Pressure Release to **Sealing**. Press **Pressure Cook**, then set the cooking time for 8 minutes.

When the cooking program is complete, press **Cancel**. Perform a quick pressure release by moving the Pressure Release to **Venting**. Open the pot and let stand for 2 minutes to cool slightly.

Set a colander in a bowl. Wearing heat-resistant mitts, lift the inner pot out of the Instant Pot housing, then pour the contents of the pot into the colander. Cover the potatoes with aluminum foil to keep warm; reserve the cooking liquid.

Wipe out the inner pot and return it to the Instant Pot housing. Press **Sauté—low** and melt the butter. Add the onion, garlic, and poblano chiles and cook, stirring occasionally, for about 5 minutes, until just softened. Pour the reserved cooking liquid into the pot, then press **Cancel**. Press **Sauté—high**. Bring to a boil and cook, stirring occasionally, for about 10 minutes, until most of the liquid evaporates.

Add the cream, then use an immersion blender to puree in the pot until smooth. Stir in the pepper. Return the potatoes to the pot, add the Anaheim chile, and stir well. Cook, stirring occasionally, for about 10 minutes, until thickened. Press **Cancel**. Taste and adjust the seasoning with salt and pepper if needed. Transfer to a serving bowl, sprinkle with the cotija and green onions (if using), and serve hot.

Serves 4 to 6

2 pounds fingerling or baby potatoes, unpeeled

1 cup vegetable broth or chicken broth

1 cup white wine

1 teaspoon kosher salt

4 tablespoons butter

½ small white onion, minced

2 large garlic cloves, minced

3 poblano chiles, roasted (see page 6), seeded, peeled, and diced

1 cup heavy cream, Mexican crema, or sour cream

1 teaspoon freshly ground black pepper

1 Anaheim chile, roasted (see page 6), seeded, peeled, and cut into thin strips

⅓ cup grated cotija cheese

2 green onions, green parts only, thinly sliced (optional)

VARIATION

For Papas con Crema y Chipotle, substitute ⅓ cup chipotle chiles in adobo sauce for the poblano chiles.

MUSHROOM "QUESOTACOS" WITH EPAZOTE

Serves 4 to 6

MUSHROOM FILLING

3 tablespoons olive oil

1 large white onion, cut into 1-inch dice (2 cups)

9 garlic cloves, minced (3 tablespoons)

½ cup water

2 teaspoons kosher salt

2 large portobello mushrooms, cut into 1-inch pieces

8 ounces cremini mushrooms, cut into quarters

8 ounces white mushrooms, cut into quarters

¼ cup shredded fresh epazote or chopped fresh cilantro leaves

½ teaspoon freshly ground black pepper

⅛ teaspoon red pepper flakes

2 poblano chiles, roasted (see page 6), seeded, peeled, and cut into ½-inch pieces

Vegetable oil for toasting the tortillas

12 corn tortillas

1¼ cups shredded Monterey Jack cheese

¾ cup grated cotija cheese

Avocado-Tomatillo Sauce (page 150) for serving

Chopped fresh cilantro for serving

The intense flavor of this mushroom filling comes from cooking down the mushrooms in their juices with smoky roasted poblanos and aromatic herbs. Use the same filling in Mushroom Enchiladas with Cheesy Chipotle Sauce (page 59), or try it in a burrito (see page 117) or tamale (see page 93). Be sure to crisp the tortillas on the griddle until *dorado*—golden brown but still chewy. A *quesotaco* is black-belt street cooking, made by browning a layer of cheese right on the griddle, scooping it up with a tortilla, and using that to wrap the delicious filling.

To make the filling: Press **Sauté—normal/medium** on the Instant Pot and heat the oil. Add the onions and cook, stirring occasionally, for about 5 minutes, until golden brown. Add the garlic and cook, stirring, for about 1 minute. Add the water, salt, portobello mushrooms, cremini mushrooms, and white mushrooms, then stir in the epazote. Press **Cancel**.

Secure the lid and set the Pressure Release to **Sealing**. Press **Pressure Cook**, then set the cooking time for 1 minute.

When the cooking program is complete, press **Cancel**. Perform a quick pressure release by moving the Pressure Release to **Venting**.

Set a colander in a bowl. Wearing heat-resistant mitts, lift the inner pot out of the Instant Pot housing, then pour the contents of the pot into the colander, reserving the liquid in the bowl. Return the inner pot to the housing, then return the cooking liquid to the pot. Press **Sauté—high**, bring the liquid to a boil, and cook for 10 to 15 minutes, until syrupy and very thick. Return the mushroom mixture to the pot and stir in the black pepper, pepper flakes, and poblano chiles. Cook, stirring occasionally, for about 3 minutes, until heated through. Taste and adjust the seasoning with salt and pepper if needed. Press **Cancel**.

Heat a cast-iron skillet or griddle over medium-high heat. Lightly oil the surface. Place a tortilla in the pan and toast for about 3 minutes, until golden brown. Turn the tortilla and top with 2 tablespoons of the Jack cheese and 1 tablespoon of the cotija cheese. Continue toasting for about 3 minutes more, until the cheese is melted and the tortilla is dorado, or crisp but flexible. Top with a few spoonfuls of the mushroom mixture, a dab of avocado-tomatillo sauce, 2 teaspoons of the remaining cotija cheese, and a pinch of cilantro. Serve right away, then toast and top the remaining tortillas in the same way, using the remaining Jack and cotija cheeses, mushroom mixture, avocado-tomatillo sauce, and cilantro.

VARIATIONS

For Grilled Corn and Mushroom "Quesotacos," add 1 cup corn kernels from 2 ears grilled corn to the pot after adding the poblano chiles.

For Inside-Out "Quesotacos," follow the recipe but use only ¾ cup of the shredded Monterey Jack. To make the "quesotacos," heat a cast-iron skillet or griddle over medium-high heat, then lightly oil the surface. Place 1 tablespoon of each type of cheese in a neat 3-inch circle directly on the hot pan, in the center. Place a tortilla on top and press firmly with a spatula. Cook for 1 to 2 minutes, until the cheese is browned. Then, using a thin metal spatula, carefully loosen the cheese from the pan and flip it with the tortilla so the browned cheese is now on top. Top with a few spoonfuls of the mushroom mixture, a dab of avocado-tomatillo sauce, 2 teaspoons of the remaining cotija cheese, and a pinch of cilantro. Serve right away, then toast and top the remaining tortillas in the same way, using the remaining Jack and cotija cheeses, mushroom mixture, avocado-tomatillo sauce, and cilantro.

PAPAS CON TOMATES Y JALAPEÑOS

Serves 4 to 6

3 Roma tomatoes, cored and cut into large pieces

6 large garlic cloves, peeled

2 teaspoons kosher salt

4 tablespoons olive oil

½ teaspoon cumin seeds

½ white onion, sliced lengthwise

3 jalapeños chiles, stemmed, seeded, and sliced

1 tablespoon tomato paste

10 fresh epazote leaves, shredded, or ¼ cup chopped fresh cilantro leaves

1 cup vegetable broth or chicken broth

2 pounds Yukon gold potatoes, peeled and cut into 1½-inch chunks

VARIATION

If you like, stir in 1 cup thawed frozen peas after opening the pot.

Flavorful but not too spicy, this vegetable *guisado* is found everywhere in Mexico, and is sometimes even transformed into a soup. The epazote leaves add a unique and authentic flavor (see page 12), but cilantro works here, too.

In a blender, combine the tomatoes, garlic, and salt. Blend until smooth, scraping down the blender as needed.

Press **Sauté—normal/medium** on the Instant Pot and heat 2 tablespoons of the oil. Add the cumin seeds and cook, stirring, for about 1 minute. Add the onion and jalapeños and cook, stirring occasionally, for about 5 minutes, until softened. Transfer the mixture to a plate.

Pour the tomato-garlic puree into the pot and cook, stirring occasionally, for 3 to 5 minutes, until all the moisture has cooked off. Add the tomato paste and epazote and cook, stirring, for about 1 minute, until the mixture is very thick and dry. Press **Cancel**. Pour in the broth and, using a wooden spoon, scrape up any browned bits on the bottom of the pot. Add the potatoes, placing them in a single layer, then place the onion mixture on top of the potatoes.

Secure the lid and set the Pressure Release to **Sealing**. Press **Pressure Cook**, then set the cooking time for 8 minutes.

When the cooking program is complete, press **Cancel**. Perform a quick pressure release by moving the Pressure Release to **Venting**. Open the pot and let stand for 10 minutes. Taste and adjust the seasoning with salt if needed.

Transfer to a serving bowl and serve hot or at room temperature, drizzled with the remaining 2 tablespoons oil.

NOTES For less spiciness, substitute 2 Anaheim chiles for the jalapeños.

Serve the stew topped with a dollop of sour cream or with a sprinkling of grated cotija cheese.

PLANTAINS WITH CHILES, LIME, AND PEANUTS

This spicy-sweet recipe will become your new favorite all-purpose side dish. The heat of the habanero is balanced by the salt, sugar, and lime, but you may substitute a less spicy chile, such as a serrano or jalapeño. Choose plantains that are yellow skinned and still very firm.

Press **Sauté—normal/medium** on the Instant Pot and melt the butter. Add the garlic, habanero chile, piloncillo (add to taste), and the lime juice. Cook, stirring constantly, for about 1 minute. Stir in the salt, water, and plantains. Press **Cancel**.

Secure the lid and set the Pressure Release to **Sealing**. Press **Pressure Cook**, then set the cooking time for 2 minutes.

When the cooking program is complete, press **Cancel**. Perform a quick pressure release by moving the Pressure Release to **Venting**. Open the pot, then press **Sauté—high**. Stir in the green onion, then bring to a boil and cook, stirring occasionally and gently, for 3 to 5 minutes, until the liquid is syrupy and the plantains are glazed.

Transfer to a serving bowl and sprinkle with the peanuts. Serve hot.

Serves 4

3 tablespoons butter

1 large garlic clove, minced (1 teaspoon)

1 habanero chile, stemmed and minced (with seeds)

1 to 2 tablespoons firmly packed crushed piloncillo (see page 12) or dark brown sugar

Juice from ½ lime

1½ teaspoons kosher salt

½ cup water or vegetable broth

3 large, firm, yellow plantains, peeled and cut into 2-inch pieces

1 green onion, white and green parts, thinly sliced

⅓ cup salted roasted peanuts, roughly chopped

NOPALES SALAD

Serves 4 to 6

1 pound nopales (see page 10)

2 cups water

1 tablespoon plus
1½ teaspoons kosher salt

Two ½-inch-thick slices from
1 white onion, plus ½ white
onion, diced

2 tablespoons olive oil

1 serrano chile, stemmed and
sliced into thin rings

¼ teaspoon dried Mexican
oregano

1 teaspoon freshly ground
black pepper

3 Roma tomatoes, cored,
seeded, and cut into
¾-inch dice

2 tablespoons fresh lime juice

¼ cup chopped fresh cilantro
leaves

½ cup coarsely crumbled
queso fresco or cotija cheese

VARIATION

For Nopales Salad with
Shrimp, add 4 ounces
frozen cooked small shrimp,
thawed, immediately before
serving.

This healthful, colorful salad made with the tender paddles of the beavertail cactus is best served warm or at room temperature. The prepared nopales will cook quickly and evenly in the Instant Pot. Then use the Sauté function to finish the warm salad right in the pot. I love this served as a taco on a warm corn tortilla.

To clean the nopales, using tongs, hold each paddle and carefully scrape off the small spines with a large knife, then trim off and discard the edges. Rinse the nopales and cut into ¾-inch squares. You should have about 4 cups.

In the Instant Pot, combine the nopales, the water, the 1 tablespoon salt, and the onion slices, then stir to combine. Secure the lid and set the Pressure Release to **Sealing**. Press **Pressure Cook**, then set the cooking time for 2 minutes.

When the cooking program is complete, press **Cancel**. Perform a quick pressure release by moving the Pressure Release to **Venting**.

Set a colander in the sink. Wearing heat-resistant mitts, lift the inner pot out of the Instant Pot housing, then pour the contents of the pot into the colander. Rinse the inner pot, wipe it dry, and return it to the Instant Pot housing. Rinse the nopales under running water, then drain again.

Press **Sauté—normal/medium** on the Instant Pot and heat the oil. Add the diced onion, the serrano chile, and the oregano, then return the nopales to the pot. Add the remaining 1½ teaspoons salt and the pepper, then cook, stirring occasionally, for about 3 minutes, until the onion is crisp-translucent. Press **Cancel**. Taste and adjust the seasoning with salt and pepper if needed.

Transfer to a serving bowl, then stir in the tomatoes, lime juice, and cilantro. Just before serving, stir in the cheese. This salad is best served at room temperature.

BURRITOS

Packed-to-the-brim burritos aren't authentically Mexican, but they are delicious. It's an excuse to fill some of our favorite Mexican-style meats and beans onto a warm flour tortilla, add cheese and salsa, roll it up, and dig in. I provide recipes and variations for a few different burrito styles below, but you can go wild. The key to a *great* burrito is making sure that everything you put into it is already hot, flavorful, juicy, and delicious. (You could assemble a burrito of cold ingredients and microwave it, but fresh and hot is so much better—really!) The ratio of fillings is nicely balanced, but you may certainly add more cheese, leave out rice, or add other salsas, inside or out. Tip: be careful not to overload the fillings or your burrito will break apart. Burritos should be consumed immediately.

The tortillas used for burritos are always flour tortillas, as they are better suited to folding and rolling than corn tortillas. Ten-inch flour tortillas, widely available in supermarkets, are a good size for burritos. If you're looking to make extra-large burritos, opt for 12- or 14-inch tortillas.

In this section, you'll find a recipe for basic beef burritos that can be tweaked to your liking. I also offer recipes for a few specific types of burritos, including "wet" burritos. Even these can be customized to suit your preferences or those of your burrito eaters.

BASIC BEEF BURRITOS

Serves 4

2 cups shredded beef plus ½ cup broth from Uno-Dos-Tres Shredded Beef and Broth (page 156)

Kosher salt

Four 10-inch flour tortillas

2 cups shredded Monterey Jack cheese, Cheddar cheese, or a combination

2 cups Arroz Rojo (page 127), hot

2 cups Refried Pinto Beans (page 124), hot

½ cup diced white onion

½ cup cored, seeded, and diced Roma tomato or Pico de Gallo (page 139)

4 tablespoons roughly chopped fresh cilantro leaves

2 ripe avocados, halved, pitted, peeled, and diced

Garnishes of your choice (see On the Table, facing page) for serving

1. In a small skillet over medium heat, combine the shredded beef and broth. Cook, stirring occasionally, for about 5 minutes, until the meat absorbs the broth; the mixture should be juicy but not wet. Taste and adjust the seasoning with salt if needed. Remove from the heat and cover to keep warm.

2. Heat a large skillet or griddle over medium heat. Add a tortilla and warm it for about 1 minute on each side, just until flexible. While the tortilla is still in the pan, scatter ½ cup of the cheese evenly over the tortilla, leaving a 1-inch margin around the sides. Transfer to a plate. Spoon on ½ cup of the hot shredded beef, leaving about a 2-inch border on each side and a 3-inch border on the top and bottom. Top the beef with ½ cup of the hot rice, ½ cup of the hot beans, 2 tablespoons of the onion, 2 tablespoons of the tomato, 1 tablespoon of the cilantro, and one-fourth of the avocado.

3. Fold the top edge of the tortilla down over the fillings, making sure it's snug against the fillings. Fold in the two sides of the tortilla to close the ends of the burrito, then roll the filled area down over the bottom edge, making sure the roll is tight and compact. Serve the burrito right away or wrap it in foil to keep it warm for a few minutes.

4. Repeat with remaining tortillas and fillings, then serve with the garnishes of your choice.

VARIATIONS

Substitute Arroz Blanco (page 134) or Arroz Verde (page 131) for the Arroz Rojo.

Substitute Cowboy Pinto Beans (page 129) or Frijoles Puercos Bean Dip (page 125) for the Refried Pinto Beans.

Add about ⅓ cup Taco Slaw (page 151) or shredded lettuce to the filling in each burrito.

In a small saucepan over low heat, warm 2 to 3 cups Red Chile Salsa (page 141), Chile Verde (page 75), Tomatillo-Chipotle Salsa (page 142), or Cheesy Chipotle Sauce (page 147). Form each burrito, then pour ½ to ¾ cup of the warm sauce over each.

CARNITAS BURRITOS

Heat a large skillet over medium heat and add the carnitas. Cook, stirring occasionally, for 5 to 7 minutes, until the meat absorbs the broth. It should be juicy but not wet. Remove from the heat and cover to keep warm.

Heat a large skillet or griddle over medium heat. Add a tortilla and warm it for about 1 minute on each side, just until flexible. Transfer to a plate. Spoon on ½ cup of the hot beans, leaving about a 2-inch border on each side and a 3-inch border on the top and bottom. Top the beans with ½ cup of the hot carnitas, one-fourth of the avocado, 2 tablespoons of the onion, 2 tablespoons of the cilantro, and 2 tablespoons of the chicharrón (if using).

Follow step 3 of Basic Beef Burritos (facing page) to wrap the tortilla around the filling.

Repeat with remaining tortillas and fillings, then serve with the salsa and the garnishes of your choice.

VARIATIONS

Roast 1 poblano chile (see page 6), then remove the seeds and skin and cut the chile into strips. Add one-fourth of the strips to the filling in each burrito.

Add about ⅓ cup Taco Slaw (page 151) to the filling in each burrito.

Serves 4

2 cups Carnitas (page 73)

Four 10-inch flour tortillas

2 cups Frijoles Puercos Bean Dip (page 125) or Cowboy Pinto Beans (page 129), hot

2 ripe avocados, halved, pitted, peeled, and diced

½ cup diced white onion

½ cup roughly chopped fresh cilantro leaves

½ cup crumbled chicharrón (see page 10; optional)

Salsa Verde (page 140) or Fresh Tomatillo Salsa (page 143)

Garnishes of your choice (see On the Table, below) for serving

ON THE TABLE

Here are some great garnishes to offer at the table:

- Habanero hot sauce (page 144)
- Pico de Gallo (page 139)
- Pickled jalapeños, homemade (page 149) or store-bought
- Sour cream or Mexican crema
- Grated cotija cheese
- Guacamole (page 150)
- Diced white onion mixed with roughly chopped fresh cilantro leaves

WET BEEF, BEAN, AND CHEESE BURRITOS

Serves 4

BURRITOS

2 cups Mexico City Short Ribs (page 62)

2 cups Basic Black Beans (page 23)

Four 10-inch flour tortillas

1⅓ cups shredded Chihuahua, Oaxacan, or Monterey Jack cheese

TOPPINGS

2 cups Ancho Chile Salsa (page 146), hot

1 cup shredded Chihuahua or Oaxacan cheese

4 tablespoons grated cotija cheese or crumbled queso fresco

4 tablespoons Mexican crema

2 ripe avocados, halved, pitted, peeled, and sliced

½ cup Pico de Gallo (page 139)

Garnishes of your choice (see On the Table, page 119) for serving

To prepare the burritos: Remove the meat from the sauce and set aside. In a skillet over medium heat, reduce the sauce from the short ribs until thick, 3 to 5 minutes, and then gently warm the meat in it, about 5 more minutes. Do not shred the meat. Remove from the heat and cover to keep warm.

In a small skillet over medium-high heat, cook the black beans for about 5 minutes, until thickened and dry. Remove from the heat and cover to keep warm.

Preheat the broiler with a rack positioned about 6 inches below the element.

Heat a large skillet or griddle over medium heat. Add a tortilla and warm it for about 1 minute on each side, just until flexible. While the tortilla is still in the pan, scatter ⅓ cup of the Chihuahua cheese on top, leaving a 1-inch margin around the sides. Transfer to a broiler-safe plate. Spoon on ½ cup of the hot beans, leaving about a 2-inch border on each side and a 3-inch border on the top and bottom. Top the beans with ½ cup of the hot beef.

Follow step 3 of Basic Beef Burritos (page 118) to wrap the tortilla around the filling; do not wrap the burrito in foil, as it will be covered with sauce and run under the broiler. Repeat with remaining tortillas, Chihuahua cheese, beans, and beef to form 3 more burritos, placing them all on a broiler-safe platter.

To top and finish the burritos: Spoon ½ cup of the hot salsa over each burrito, then sprinkle each with ¼ cup of the Chihuahua cheese and 1 tablespoon of the cotija cheese. Broil for about 3 minutes, until the cheese is melted and bubbly.

Remove from the broiler and carefully transfer to individual plates. Drizzle each burrito 1 tablespoon of the crema, then top with one-fourth of the avocado and 2 tablespoons of the pico de gallo.

Serve right away with the garnishes of your choice.

CALIFORNIA FAJITA BURRITOS

In a skillet over medium-high heat, warm the oil. Add the onion, garlic, Anaheim chiles, jalapeños, and red bell pepper. Cook, stirring occasionally, for about 2 minutes, until crisp-tender. Add the salt, cumin, pepper flakes, and black pepper and cook, stirring, for about 2 minutes, until the vegetables are softened. Stir in the tomatoes and cilantro and cook for about 1 minute, until heated through. Transfer to a plate and cover with aluminum foil to keep warm.

To the same skillet, add the beef and broth. Cook over medium-high heat, stirring occasionally, for 3 to 5 minutes, until the meat absorbs the broth; the mixture should be juicy but not wet. Taste and adjust the seasoning with salt if needed. Remove from the heat and cover to keep warm.

Heat a large skillet or griddle over medium heat. Add a tortilla and warm it for about 1 minute on each side, just until flexible. While the tortilla is still in the pan, scatter ½ cup of the cheese on top, leaving a 1-inch margin around the sides. Transfer to a plate. Spoon on ½ cup of the hot beans, leaving about a 2-inch border on each side and a 3-inch border on the top and bottom. Top the beans with one-fourth of the cooked vegetables, ½ cup of the hot beef, ¼ cup of the guacamole, and 1 slice of bacon (if using).

Follow step 3 of Basic Beef Burritos (page 118) to wrap the tortilla around the filling.

Repeat with remaining tortillas and fillings, then serve with the garnishes of your choice.

Serves 4

1½ tablespoons vegetable oil

1 red onion, thinly sliced

6 garlic cloves, minced (2 tablespoons)

2 Anaheim chiles, stemmed, seeded, and cut into strips

1 or 2 jalapeño chiles, stemmed, seeded (optional), and cut into strips

1 red bell pepper, stemmed, seeded, and cut into strips

2 teaspoons kosher salt

1 teaspoon ground cumin

1 teaspoon red pepper flakes

½ teaspoon freshly ground black pepper

2 Roma tomatoes, cored, seeded, and cut into strips

Leaves from ½ bunch cilantro, chopped

2 cups shredded beef and ⅓ cup broth (page 156) or 2 cups shredded chicken and ⅓ cup broth (page 154) from Uno-Dos-Tres recipe

Four 10-inch flour tortillas

2 cups shredded pepper Jack cheese

2 cups Refried Pinto Beans (page 124), hot

1 cup Guacamole (page 150), plus more for serving

4 slices bacon, cooked until crisp (optional)

Garnishes of your choice (see On the Table, page 119) for serving

chapter 5

RICE
&
BEANS

REFRIED PINTO BEANS

Serves 6 to 8

2 cups dried pinto beans

2 tablespoons vegetable oil

1 cup diced white or yellow onion

3 garlic cloves, chopped (1 tablespoon)

2 guajillo or California chiles, stemmed, seeded, and torn into pieces

3 chiles de árbol, or ½ teaspoon red pepper flakes

1 bay leaf

1 teaspoon dried Mexican oregano

1 teaspoon freshly ground black pepper

6 cups water

1 tablespoon kosher salt

2 tablespoons bacon fat, pork fat from Carnitas (page 73), or vegetable oil

Crumbled cotija cheese for serving

Thinly sliced green onions, green parts only, for serving

Pico de Gallo (page 139) for serving

Refried beans are essential to Mexican cuisine. With the Instant Pot, they come out perfect every time, and you won't have to watch over them for hours. Presoak the beans for a creamier texture. If you don't, the cooking time may vary, depending on their age. The beans will appear soupy after cooking, but they will absorb some of the liquid and thicken as they cool.

Place the beans in a large bowl, cover with 6 cups water, and let soak overnight at room temperature. Drain the beans.

Press **Sauté—normal/medium** on the Instant Pot and heat the oil. Add the onion, garlic, guajillo chiles, árbol chiles, bay, oregano,and pepper. Cook, stirring occasionally, for about 5 minutes, until the onion begins to soften. Add the drained beans, the water, and the salt, then stir to combine. Press **Cancel**.

Secure the lid and set the Pressure Release to **Sealing**. Press **Beans**, then set the cooking time for 30 minutes.

When the cooking program is complete, press **Cancel**. Let the pressure release naturally for 30 minutes, then move the Pressure Release to **Venting** to release any remaining steam.

Open the pot—the beans will appear very soupy at this point. Let cool to room temperature; the beans will absorb quite a bit of the liquid during cooling.

Reserve 1 cup of the cooking liquid. Using an immersion blender, puree the beans and the remaining cooking liquid directly in the pot until smooth. Alternatively, working in batches if necessary, transfer to a regular blender and puree until smooth, then return to the pot.

Add the bacon fat to the pureed beans. Press **Sauté—high** on the Instant Pot and cook the beans, stirring frequently and scraping the bottom of the pot, until thickened but still moist; this may take up to 30 minutes.

If the beans are too thick for your taste, thin them with the reserved cooking liquid to the desired consistency. Taste and adjust the seasoning with salt and pepper if needed. Sprinkle with cotija cheese and green onions and serve pico de gallo on the side.

NOTES If you're cooking unsoaked beans, set the cooking time for 35 minutes. Let the pressure release naturally for 30 minutes, then move the Pressure Release to **Venting** to release any remaining steam. Open the pot and taste a bean. If it is dry or crumbly inside, secure the lid again and the Pressure Release to **Sealing**. Press **Pressure Cook**, then set the cooking time for 5 minutes. Perform a quick pressure release by moving the Pressure Release to **Venting**. Open the pot and test again.

VARIATIONS

For **Borracho Beans**, add ½ cup beer to the beans while pureeing.

For **Frijoles Puercos Bean Dip**, stir an ½ teaspoon freshly ground black pepper and ⅓ cup bacon fat or pork fat from Carnitas into the refried beans. Spoon into a broiler-safe baking dish and top with a good handful of shredded Monterey Jack cheese. Broil until the cheese is melted and bubbly. Top with a drizzle of sour cream and a sprinkle of grated cotija cheese, diced white onion, chopped fresh cilantro leaves, and crumbled chicharrón. Serve with tortilla chips or tostadas for dipping.

For **Frijoles Maneados**, cook the pureed beans until very thick, then stir in ¼ cup heavy cream, 1 tablespoon butter, and 2 tablespoons cream cheese. Spread in a 6-cup broiler-safe baking dish. Top with ⅓ shredded Monterey Jack or Chihuahua cheese. Broil until the cheese is melted and bubbly. Serve with tortilla chips.

DRESS YOUR BEANS

Well-made beans are delicious all by themselves, but they take readily to dressing up with different garnishes and toppings. Here are some ideas to get you started.

- **Crumbled queso fresco**
- **Grated cotija cheese**
- **Mexican crema**
- **Pico de Gallo (page 139)**
- **Pickled Jalapeños and Carrots (page 149)**
- **Nopales Salad (page 114)**
- **Carnitas (page 73)**
- **Crumbled chicharrón**
- **Sliced green onions, green parts only**
- **Diced white onion and chopped fresh cilantro leaves mixed in equal parts**
- **Sofrito** In a small skillet over medium-high heat, warm 1 tablespoon vegetable oil. Add ¼ cup diced white onion and cook, stirring frequently, for about 5 minutes, until golden brown. Stir in 1 teaspoon minced garlic, ½ cup seeded and diced Roma tomato, and with ¼ teaspoon kosher salt and use as a topping.

ARROZ ROJO (RED RICE)

Lightly frying the rice in a puree of aromatic fresh vegetables infuses every grain of rice with flavor. Because of the intense, moist heat in the Instant Pot, it's important to use a Natural Release so the rice finishes cooking evenly. It will appear very soft when the lid is opened, but as it rests, uncovered, it will firm up. See Arroz Perfecto (page 130) for more tips.

In a blender, combine the tomato, tomatillo, and salt. Blend until liquefied. Add the onion, garlic, tomato paste, and jalapeño (if using) and blend until smooth, scraping down the blender as needed.

Press **Sauté—normal/medium** on the Instant Pot and heat the oil. Add the rice and cook, stirring frequently, for 3 to 5 minutes, until light golden brown. Pour in the tomato-onion puree and cook, stirring occasionally, for about 3 minutes, until the rice has absorbed most of the liquid. Press **Cancel**.

Pour the broth into the blender, swish it around to loosen any residual puree, then stir the broth into the rice mixture. Wearing heat-resistant mitts, lift the inner pot out of the Instant Pot housing and gently swirl the inner pot to get the grains to settle into an even layer. Return the inner pot to the housing.

Secure the lid and set the Pressure Release to **Sealing**. Press **Pressure Cook**, then set the cooking time for 8 minutes.

When the cooking program is complete, press **Cancel**. Let the pressure release naturally for 10 minutes, then move the Pressure Release to **Venting** to release any remaining steam. Open the pot, then, using a fork or chopsticks, gently fluff the rice. Stir in the cilantro and let rest, uncovered, for 5 minutes. Serve hot.

Serves 4 to 6

1 large Roma tomato, cored and cut into quarters

1 tomatillo, husked and roughly chopped

1 tablespoon kosher salt

¼ white onion, roughly chopped

1 large garlic clove, peeled

2 tablespoons tomato paste

½ jalapeño chile, stemmed and seeded (optional)

1 tablespoon vegetable oil

2 cups long-grain white rice, rinsed and drained

1½ cups chicken broth

¼ cup roughly chopped fresh cilantro leaves

COWBOY PINTO BEANS

This is true cowboy cooking—flavorful, filling, and spicy, and a meal in one pot. Pork aficionados will want to top the beans with pork belly, carnitas, or chorizo. Make a meal of it with some warm corn tortillas, or turn it into a soup (page 21), or add to a burrito (see page 119).

Place the beans in a large bowl, cover with 6 cups water, and let soak overnight at room temperature. Drain the beans.

Press **Sauté—high** on the Instant Pot. Add the oil, bacon, and pork hock and cook, stirring, for about 5 minutes, until the bacon has rendered its fat and is lightly browned. Add the garlic, onion, California chile, pepper, and oregano and cook, stirring, for 1 minute. Add the water, salt, epazote, chipotle chiles, and the tomatoes and their liquid.

Secure the lid and set the Pressure Release to **Sealing**. Press **Beans**, then set the cooking time for 30 minutes.

When the cooking program is complete, press **Cancel**. Let the pressure release naturally for 30 minutes, then move the Pressure Release to **Venting** to release any remaining steam.

Open the pot and transfer the pork hock to a plate. Taste a bean—it should be creamy and tender. If it is not, secure the lid once again and set the Pressure Release to **Sealing**. Press **Pressure Cook**, then set the cooking time for 5 minutes. When the cooking program is complete, press **Cancel**. Let the pressure release naturally for 20 minutes, then move the Pressure Release to **Venting** to release any remaining steam. Open the pot and taste another bean.

CONTINUED

Serves 6 to 8

2 cups dried pinto beans

2 tablespoons vegetable oil

1 slice thick-cut bacon, diced

1 smoked pork hock or smoked turkey thigh (about 12 ounces)

6 garlic cloves, sliced (about 2 tablespoons)

½ large white or yellow onion, diced

1 California or guajillo chile, stemmed, seeded, and broken into pieces

1 tablespoon freshly ground black pepper

2 teaspoons dried Mexican oregano

6 cups water or vegetable broth

4 teaspoons kosher salt

10 fresh epazote leaves, shredded, or ¼ cup roughly chopped fresh cilantro leaves

4 chipotle chiles in adobo sauce, minced

One 14½-ounce can diced tomatoes and their liquid, or 3 Roma tomatoes, cored and diced

2 poblano or Anaheim chiles, roasted (see page 6), seeded, peeled, and diced

Remove and discard the skin and bones from the pork hock and shred the meat into bite-size pieces. Stir the shredded meat and the poblanos into the beans. Taste and adjust the seasoning with salt and pepper if needed. If you want a thicker consistency, use a potato masher to break up some of the beans.

NOTES If you forget to soak your beans, cook them for 35 minutes and allow the pressure to release naturally for 30 minutes, then taste one for doneness. If it is dry or crumbly, secure the lid and set the Pressure Release to **Sealing**. Press **Pressure Cook**, then set the cooking time for 5 minutes. Perform a quick pressure release by moving the **Pressure Release** to **Venting**.

For spicier beans, increase the chipotle chiles in adobo sauce to 5 chiles, minced, or add ½ teaspoon red pepper flakes along with the chipotles.

Serve the beans with a sprinkle of crumbled cotija cheese or a dollop of Mexican crema.

ARROZ PERFECTO

Mexican rice recipes start by frying the rice with a puree of aromatics and fresh vegetables, which adds great fresh flavor as well as nutritional value. And you can do it all right in the Instant Pot, which will ensure perfect results every time. Here are some tips for cooking perfect rice.

· **Don't substitute brown rice for the long-grain white rice called for in the recipes. Brown rice requires a different liquid amount and cooking time.**

· *Always* **rinse and drain rice well before cooking. I use a large wire-mesh strainer, a great kitchen tool that's also useful for straining sauces, moles, and broths.**

· **Sautéing the rice in a small amount of vegetable oil before adding the liquid yields grains that cook up separate and distinct.**

· **For even more special rice, use homemade chicken broth instead of water.**

· **A natural pressure release and final rest are essential for perfect results. Don't skip them.**

· **Use a fork or chopsticks to gently fluff the cooked grains before the final rest.**

· **For best results, do not double recipes.**

Leftover rice can be frozen in freezer bags for up to 1 month. To reheat, thaw overnight in the refrigerator, then place in a microwave-safe bowl and microwave on high until hot. Alternatively, place the rice in a saucepan along with a small amount of water or broth, cover, and warm over low heat until hot.

ARROZ VERDE (GREEN RICE)

I always keep a few roasted poblanos in my freezer, just so I can make this wonderful green rice on a whim. It's my all-time favorite for dressing up a simple roast chicken or grilled fish dinner. It's terrific in any burrito (see page 118) or with *albóndigas* (page 76). And you can use it to make stuffed chiles (page 106). See Arroz Perfecto (page 130) for more tips.

In a blender, combine the poblano chiles, jalapeño, onion, garlic, tomatillo, salt, and water. Blend until smooth, scraping down the blender as needed.

Press **Sauté—normal/medium** on the Instant Pot and heat the oil. Add the rice and cook, stirring frequently, for 3 to 5 minutes, until lightly golden brown. Pour in the chile puree and cook, stirring occasionally, for about 5 minutes, until all the liquid is absorbed. Press **Cancel**.

Add the broth to the rice mixture. Wearing heat-resistant mitts, lift the inner pot out of the Instant Pot housing and gently swirl the inner pot to get the grains to settle into an even layer. Return the inner pot to the housing.

Secure the lid and set the Pressure Release to **Sealing**. Press **Pressure Cook**, then set the cooking time for 15 minutes.

When the cooking program is complete, press **Cancel**. Let the pressure release naturally for 10 minutes, then move the Pressure Release to **Venting** to release any remaining steam. Open the pot, then, using a fork or chopsticks, gently fluff the rice. Stir in the cilantro and let rest, uncovered, for 10 to 15 minutes. Taste and adjust the seasoning with salt if needed. Serve hot.

VARIATION

For a vegan version, substitute vegetable broth or water for the chicken stock.

Serves 4 to 6

2 poblano or Anaheim chiles, roasted (see page 6), seeded, and peeled

1 large jalapeño chile, stemmed and seeded

½ small white or yellow onion, roughly chopped

3 large garlic cloves, peeled

1 tomatillo, husked and roughly chopped

2 teaspoons kosher salt

½ cup water

2 tablespoons vegetable oil

2 cups long-grain white rice, rinsed and drained

1½ cups chicken broth

Leaves from ½ bunch cilantro, finely chopped

RICE WITH SEAFOOD

Serves 4

1 cup dry white wine, such as Sauvignon Blanc

1 teaspoon saffron threads

3 tablespoons olive oil

6 garlic cloves, minced (2 tablespoons)

8 ounces medium shrimp, peeled and deveined

4 ounces thick, firm, skinless white fish fillets, such as halibut or sea bass, cut into 1-inch pieces

6 ounces cleaned small squid, sliced, or 6 ounces sea scallops, cut into quarters

12 mussels, scrubbed and debearded

3 teaspoons kosher salt

½ small white or yellow onion, diced

½ red bell pepper, stemmed, seeded, and sliced

½ green bell pepper, stemmed, seeded, and sliced

1 serrano chile, stemmed, seeded, and minced

2 Roma tomatoes, cored, seeded, and diced

2 teaspoons smoked paprika

1 tablespoon tomato paste

2½ cups long-grain white rice, rinsed and drained

This savory rice and seafood dish (*arroz con mariscos*) is much more forgiving than paella, especially when made in the Instant Pot. This is one of the easiest, most impressive, *and* most delicious recipes in this book. Be sure to rinse the rice before cooking (see Arroz Perfecto page 130).

In a small saucepan, bring the wine to a bare simmer over medium-high heat. Alternatively, place the wine in a microwave-safe bowl and microwave on high for about 30 seconds, until hot. Add the saffron threads to the warm wine and let steep for about 30 minutes.

Press **Sauté—normal/medium** on the Instant Pot and heat 1 tablespoon of the oil. Add the garlic and shrimp and cook, stirring occasionally, for 2 to 3 minutes, until the shrimp are pink. Transfer to a plate. Add the fish and cook, stirring carefully, for 2 to 3 minutes, until opaque, then transfer to the plate. Add the squid and cook, stirring occasionally, for 2 to 3 minutes, until opaque, then transfer to the plate. Finally, add the mussels and cook, stirring occasionally, for about 3 minutes, until the mussels have opened, then transfer to the plate, discarding any mussels that have not opened. Press **Cancel**. Season the seafood with 1 teaspoon of the salt. Wearing heat-resistant mitts, lift out the inner pot from the Instant Pot housing and pour the juices over the seafood. Return the inner pot to the housing. Cover the seafood with aluminum foil to keep warm.

Press **Sauté—normal/medium** on the Instant Pot and heat the remaining 2 tablespoons oil. Add the onion, red bell pepper, green bell pepper, serrano chile, and tomatoes. Cook, stirring occasionally, for about 2 minutes, until just softened.

Add the remaining 2 teaspoons salt, the smoked paprika, and the tomato paste. Cook, stirring, for about 2 minutes. Stir in the rice, chicken broth, and seafood stock.

Secure the lid and set the Pressure Release to **Sealing**. Press **Pressure Cook**, then set the cooking time for 8 minutes.

When the cooking program is complete, press **Cancel**. Let the pressure release naturally for 10 minutes, then move the Pressure Release to **Venting** to release any remaining steam. Open the pot, then use a fork to gently fluff the rice. Add the seafood and any accumulated juices and the cilantro, then stir gently to combine. Replace the lid without securing it and let rest for 10 minutes.

Serve the rice hot with lemon wedges on the side.

NOTE If you don't have seafood stock, clam juice, or Clamato, simply use an additional 1 cup chicken broth.

1 cup chicken broth

1 cup seafood stock, clam juice, or Clamato

¼ cup chopped fresh cilantro leaves

Lemon wedges for serving

ARROZ BLANCO (WHITE RICE)

Serves 4 to 6

2 tablespoons vegetable oil

½ small white or yellow onion, minced

3 garlic cloves, minced (about 1 tablespoon)

2 cups long-grain white rice, rinsed and drained

2 teaspoons kosher salt

1¼ cups water

1 cup chicken broth

I admit to being a rice klutz. But with the Instant Pot, I finally have a foolproof and forgiving system for producing amazing rice every time. The keys to success are rinsing and draining the rice before cooking, using homemade broth, and allowing the rice to rest after cooking. See Arroz Perfecto (page 130) for more tips.

Press **Sauté—normal/medium** on the Instant Pot and heat the oil. Add the onion and garlic and cook, stirring constantly, for about 1 minute, until lightly browned. Add the rice and cook, stirring, for about 2 minutes, until the grains begin to take on a light golden tinge. Press **Cancel**. Add the salt, water, and broth, then scrape up any rice that may be stuck to the bottom or sides of the pot. Wearing heat-resistant mitts, lift the inner pot out of the Instant Pot housing and gently swirl the inner pot to get the grains to settle into an even layer. Return the inner pot to the housing.

Secure the lid and set the Pressure Release to **Sealing**. Press **Rice**.

When the cooking program is complete, press **Cancel**. Let the pressure release naturally for 10 minutes, then move the Pressure Release to **Venting** to release any remaining steam. Open the pot and, using a fork or chopsticks, gently fluff the rice. Wipe off the condensation from the lid, then replace it without securing it. Let the rice rest for 10 minutes. Serve hot.

VARIATIONS

For rice with fresh tomato, add 2 Roma tomatoes, cored, seeded, and diced, while the rice rests.

For Lemon-Herb Rice, stir in the juice of 1 lemon and about 2 tablespoons chopped fresh cilantro, basil, or flat-leaf parsley leaves, just before the rice rests.

For long-grain brown rice, use 1¼ cups each chicken broth and water (for a total of 2½ cups liquid) and cook on **Pressure Cook** for 15 minutes.

QUINOA CON PASAS

This quinoa dish is enhanced with citrus-infused raisins (*pasas*) and the crunch of toasted *pepitas*. It may be served hot, at room temperature, or cold. Like rice, quinoa must be thoroughly rinsed and drained before cooking.

Serves 4 to 6

½ cup raisins
Juice of ½ orange
Juice of ½ lemon
1 tablespoon cider vinegar
1 cup quinoa, rinsed and drained
2 cups water
1 teaspoon kosher salt
1 teaspoon olive oil
¼ cup roughly chopped cilantro leaves
¼ cup pepitas (shelled pumpkin seeds), toasted

In a small bowl, stir together the raisins, orange juice, lemon juice, and vinegar. Set aside.

In the Instant Pot, stir together the quinoa, water, salt, and oil. Secure the lid and set the Pressure Release to **Sealing**. Press **Pressure Cook**, then set the cooking time for 1 minute.

When the cooking program is complete, press **Cancel**. Perform a quick pressure release by moving the Pressure Release to **Venting**. Do not open the pot and let rest for 10 minutes.

Open the pot, then use a fork to gently fluff the quinoa. Add the raisins and any juices and the cilantro and stir gently to combine. Let rest uncovered for 5 minutes. Taste and adjust the seasoning with salt if needed. Transfer to a serving bowl and sprinkle with the pepitas.

NOTES If you like, substitute dried cranberries for the raisins.
You can also substitute 1 tablespoon tequila for the cider vinegar.

chapter 6

ESSENTIALS

PICO DE GALLO

Mildly spicy, crunchy, and fresh, pico de gallo doesn't require any cooking. It is a go-to finish for tacos and is great on burritos, refried beans, and even to top off a soup. To vary the flavor, add a bit of diced mango.

In a small bowl, stir together all of the ingredients. Taste and adjust the salt if needed; the salsa should be well seasoned. Serve right away or cover and refrigerate for up to 1 day.

VARIATION

To make *xni-pec*, a spicy Yucatecan salsa, substitute a habanero chile for the jalapeño and stir in a dash of cider vinegar at the end.

Makes 2 cups

3 Roma tomatoes, cored, seeded, and cut into ¼-inch dice (about 1½ cups)

½ cup finely diced white or red onion

1 small jalapeño or serrano chile, stemmed and minced

1 tablespoon minced fresh cilantro leaves

1 tablespoon fresh lime juice

¾ teaspoon kosher salt

SALSA VERDE

Makes 3½ cups

1 pound tomatillos (about 10), husked

½ white onion, diced

2 garlic cloves, peeled

1 large jalapeño chile, stemmed and seeded

1 cup water

1 teaspoon kosher salt

1 whole clove

Leaves from ½ bunch cilantro, roughly chopped

Slightly tart and vibrantly green, *salsa verde* is one of *the* essential Mexican salsas, and it couldn't be faster or easier. Use it with anything pork, chicken, or cheese. It's a key ingredient in Pork Albóndigas in Green Sauce with Chicharrón (page 76).

In the Instant Pot, combine the tomatillos, onion, garlic, jalapeño, water, salt, and clove. Secure the lid and set the Pressure Release to **Sealing**. Press **Pressure Cook**, then set the cooking time for 3 minutes.

When the cooking program is complete, press **Cancel**. Perform a quick pressure release by moving the Pressure Release to **Venting**. Open the pot, then add the cilantro. Using an immersion blender, puree the mixture directly in the pot until smooth. Cover and refrigerate for up to 3 days or freeze for up to 3 months.

WHY FRY A SALSA?

Technique is what makes the difference in authentic Mexican cooking. One important technique is frying a chile puree in a small amount of fat to develop and concentrate flavors as you stir (and stir, and stir), cooking off excess liquid, changing the color, and dramatically changing the final taste. This is an essential step in all moles and in several of the *guisados*, such as Oaxacan Chileajo (page 86.) Use a deep, narrow pot (the Instant Pot is ideal, if not otherwise occupied) and a splatter guard, as the chile paste will throw lava-like splatters as it thickens.

RED CHILE SALSA

This classic enchilada sauce is useful for many dishes, in addition to enchiladas. I add it to tamale masa (see page 96), pour it over burritos (see page 118), and stir it into a tamale filling. It is used in several other recipes in this book, notably Chicken Enchilada Soup (page 25) and Mexico City short ribs (page 62). And it cooks up in the Instant Pot in about 15 minutes.

Press **Sauté—normal/medium** on the Instant Pot and heat the oil. Add the chiles and cook, stirring frequently, for about 2 minutes, until just softened. Add the onion, garlic, tomatoes, oregano, cumin, clove, and pepper and cook, stirring occasionally, for 3 to 5 minutes, until the onion has softened. Press **Cancel**. Stir in the water and salt.

Secure the lid and set the Pressure Release to **Sealing**. Press **Pressure Cook—normal**, then set the cooking time for 5 minutes.

When the cooking program is complete, press **Cancel**. Perform a quick pressure release by moving the Pressure Release to **Venting**. Open the pot and let cool for 5 minutes.

Set a wire-mesh strainer over a large bowl. Working in batches, puree the mixture in a blender until very, very smooth, then pour the puree into the strainer. Discard the solids left in the strainer.

Transfer the salsa to an airtight container or containers and let cool to room temperature. Cover and refrigerate for up to 3 days or freeze for up to 3 months.

NOTES The salsa is mildly spicy. To make it spicier, substitute guajillo chiles for the California chiles or add 1 chile de árbol.

If the sauce separates after freezing and thawing, give it a quick whirl in the blender.

Makes 6 cups

1 tablespoon vegetable oil

16 California chiles, stemmed, seeded, and torn into pieces (3½ to 4 cups, packed)

1 small white or yellow onion, diced (about 1 cup)

4 large garlic cloves, sliced

2 Roma tomatoes, cored and diced

1 teaspoon dried Mexican oregano leaves

½ teaspoon ground cumin

1 whole clove

½ teaspoon freshly ground black pepper

6 cups water or chicken broth

1 tablespoon kosher salt

TOMATILLO-CHIPOTLE SALSA

Makes 4 ½ cups

1 tablespoon vegetable oil

4 large garlic cloves, peeled

1 cup white or yellow onion, diced

1 pound tomatillos (about 10), husked and roughly chopped

4 Roma tomatoes, cored and cut into quarters

½ cup water

2½ teaspoons kosher salt

¼ cup chipotles chiles in adobo sauce

¼ cup chopped fresh cilantro leaves

This all-purpose salsa gets a smoky hit from the chipotles in adobo. It comes together in minutes and can be blended right in the Instant Pot. Serve as a table salsa for dipping chips, spooning over a burrito (see page 118), or as a substitute for any salsa in this book.

Press **Sauté—normal/medium** on the Instant Pot and heat the oil. Add garlic and onion and cook, stirring, for about 1 minute. Add the tomatillos and tomatoes and cook, stirring occasionally, for about 2 minutes, until barely softened. Press **Cancel**. Stir in the water and salt.

Secure the lid and set the Pressure Release to **Sealing**. Press **Pressure Cook**, then set the cooking time for 3 minutes.

When the cooking program is complete, press **Cancel**. Perform a quick pressure release by moving the Pressure Release to **Venting**.

Open the pot, then add the chipotle chiles. Using an immersion blender, puree the mixture directly in the pot until almost smooth—a little texture is okay. Alternatively, transfer the mixture to a regular blender and pulse a few times. (The contents are hot, so don't fill your blender more than half full and pulse carefully. You may need to do it in batches.) Add the cilantro and pulse a few times to combine. Taste and adjust the seasoning with salt if needed.

Cover and refrigerate for up to 3 days or freeze for up to 3 months.

NOTES For a more tomatoey salsa, use only 8 ounces tomatillos and increase the tomatoes to 6. You can also add ¼ teaspoon dried Mexican oregano along with the garlic and onion.

FRESH TOMATILLO SALSA

Cooked *salsa verde* (page 140) is common, but this version, made with raw tomatillos, adds a hit of fresh tartness and a bit of heat to any rich or fatty foods, such as carnitas, eggs, steak or shrimp, and anything with cheese.

Makes about 1½ cups

8 ounces tomatillos, husked and roughly chopped

⅓ white onion, roughly chopped

1 or 2 serrano chiles, stemmed

Leaves from 6 sprigs cilantro

1¼ teaspoons kosher salt

In a food processor, combine all of the ingredients and pulse until fairly smooth, about 10 pulses. The salsa should not be perfectly smooth. Transfer to a bowl, then taste and adjust the seasoning with salt if needed; the salsa should be seasoned assertively.

Serve right away or cover and refrigerate for up to 24 hours. Before serving, taste and adjust the seasoning with salt if needed.

VARIATION

To make Tomatillo-Pineapple Salsa, add ¼ cup cut-up fresh pineapple to the food processor with the other ingredients.

HABANERO HOT SAUCE #1

Makes 2 cups

1½ cups water

1 cup chiles de árbol, stemmed

3 habanero chiles, stemmed

2 large garlic cloves, peeled

1½ teaspoons kosher salt

2 teaspoons cider vinegar

No Mexican table is complete without a fiery hot sauce. Add it in small quantities to adjust the heat level of your food to your liking. These two sauces are very different—#1 is tangy with a dash of vinegar, and #2 is just plain hot.

In the Instant Pot, combine the water, árbol chiles, habanero chiles, garlic, and salt. Secure the lid and set the Pressure Release to **Sealing**. Press **Pressure Cook**, then set the cooking time for 5 minutes.

When the cooking program is complete, press **Cancel**. Perform a quick pressure release by moving the Pressure Release to **Venting**. Open the pot, then transfer the contents of the pot to a blender. Add the vinegar and blend until smooth.

Transfer to a clean jar or jars, cover tightly, and refrigerate for up to 1 week.

HABANERO HOT SAUCE #2

Makes 2 cups

1 cup water

4 Roma tomatoes, cored

3 habanero chiles, stemmed

1 teaspoon kosher salt

In the Instant Pot, combine all of the ingredients. Secure the lid and set the Pressure Release to Sealing. Press Pressure Cook, then set the cooking time for 4 minutes.

When the cooking program is complete, press **Cancel**. Perform a quick pressure release by moving the Pressure Release to **Venting**. Transfer the contents of the pot to a blender and blend until smooth.

Transfer to a clean jar or jars, cover tightly, and refrigerate for up to 1 week.

ANCHO CHILE SALSA

Makes 4 cups

1 tablespoon vegetable oil

3 ancho chiles, stemmed, seeded, and torn into pieces

3 guajillo chiles, stemmed, seeded, and torn into pieces

1 small white or yellow onion, diced

2 large garlic cloves, sliced

1 Roma tomato, cored and cut into quarters

5 tomatillos, husked and roughly chopped

1 teaspoon kosher salt

½ teaspoon freshly ground black pepper

½ teaspoon dried Mexican oregano

2 cups water

This excellent, all-purpose salsa is used in Chicken in Ancho Chile Salsa (page 45) but is also a great option for enchiladas, over burritos, for bathing stuffed poblano chiles (page 106), for serving with eggs and tortillas, or used as a substitute for Red Chile Salsa (page 141) in any recipe. The combination of dried chiles with tomatillos delivers tanginess and complexity.

———————

Press **Sauté—normal/medium** on the Instant Pot and heat the oil. Add the ancho chiles, guajillo chiles, onion, and garlic and cook, stirring occasionally, for about 2 minutes, until the onion has softened. Add the tomato, tomatillos, salt, pepper, and oregano and cook, stirring, for about 2 minutes, until slightly softened. Press **Cancel**. Stir in the water.

Secure the lid and set the Pressure Release to **Sealing**. Press **Pressure Cook-normal**, then set the cooking time for 5 minutes.

When the cooking program is complete, press **Cancel**. Perform a quick pressure release by moving the Pressure Release to **Venting**. Open the pot and let cool for 5 minutes.

Using an immersion blender, puree the mixture directly in the pot until fairly smooth, with some flecks of chiles.

The salsa may be stored in the refrigerator, covered, for up to 3 days.

CHEESY CHIPOTLE SAUCE

This is a great sauce to have in your repertoire as a changeup from more traditional recipes. Use it on enchiladas (see page 59) and burritos (see page 118), and even over turkey or chicken. Cream sauces can be finicky, but the Instant Pot's controlled, even heat guarantees a great result. Make this sauce as spicy as you like by adding more (or less) chipotles in adobo.

Makes 4 cups

1 tablespoon olive oil

2 tablespoons butter

½ small white or yellow onion, minced

3 large garlic cloves, minced

3 large chipotle chiles in adobo sauce, minced to a paste

3 tablespoons all-purpose flour

1 cup chicken broth

1 tablespoon kosher salt

1½ teaspoons freshly ground black pepper

1½ cups whole milk

½ cup heavy cream

2 tablespoons cream cheese

1½ cups shredded medium-aged Cheddar cheese

¼ cup grated cotija cheese

Press **Sauté—normal/medium** on the Instant Pot and heat the oil and butter. When the butter has melted, add the onion, garlic, and chipotle chiles and cook, stirring frequently, for about 5 minutes, until the onion is softened. Add the flour and cook, stirring and scraping along the bottom of the pot, for about 1 minute. Whisk in the broth, salt, and pepper and bring to a simmer, whisking constantly. Whisk in the milk and cream and cook, stirring frequently, for 5 minutes, until the mixture is smooth and thick. Whisk in the cream cheese until smooth. Press **Cancel**.

Set a wire-mesh strainer over a bowl. Wearing heat-resistant mitts, lift the inner pot out of the Instant Pot housing and pour the sauce into the strainer. Add the Cheddar and cotija to the strained sauce and whisk until smooth. Serve warm.

Store leftovers in an airtight container in the refrigerator for up to 1 day; to serve, reheat gently in a small saucepan over low heat, stirring frequently.

VARIATIONS

Top whatever you are serving with the sauce with chopped fresh cilantro leaves or finely sliced green onion tops.

Add sautéed mushrooms and serve alongside Tequila-Brined Turkey (page 50) and rice.

PICKLED JALAPEÑOS AND CARROTS

This essential spicy, tangy hit for tacos is also great in sandwiches, on burgers, in salads, or just to snack on. Because the carrots absorb the heat infused into the cooking liquid by the chiles, they tend to be hotter than the chiles. Want them still hotter? Throw in a couple of split habaneros. The ingredients list is long, but the cooking time in the Instant Pot is very short—less than 10 minutes.

Press **Sauté—normal/medium** on the Instant Pot and heat the oil. Add the carrots, onion, garlic, salt, peppercorns, oregano, coriander seeds, cloves, allspice, bay, and cinnamon. Cook, stirring occasionally, for about 5 minutes, until fragrant. Add the jalapeños, habaneros (if using), cider vinegar, and white vinegar, then stir to combine.

Secure the lid and set the Pressure Release to **Sealing**. Press **Pressure Cook**, then set the cooking time for 2 minutes.

When the cooking program is complete, press **Cancel**. Perform a quick pressure release by moving the Pressure Release to **Venting**. Open the pot and stir in the agave syrup. Let cool to room temperature.

Transfer the pickles with their brine to glass jars. Cover and refrigerate for up to 1 month.

NOTE Try adding other firm, raw vegetables in place of the carrots, such as 1 cup small cauliflower florets or 1 cup peeled and cubed chayote.

Makes about 4 cups

2 tablespoons olive oil

4 large carrots, peeled and sliced 1 inch thick on a sharp diagonal

½ white onion, sliced ½ inch thick

4 large garlic cloves, sliced

1 tablespoon kosher salt

1 teaspoon black peppercorns, lightly crushed

1 teaspoon dried Mexican oregano

1 teaspoon coriander seeds, lightly crushed

6 whole cloves

3 allspice berries, lightly crushed

2 bay leaves

One 1-inch piece cinnamon stick

1 pound jalapeño chiles (about 10), with stems

2 habanero chiles, stemmed and halved (optional)

2 cups cider vinegar

1 cup distilled white vinegar

2 tablespoons agave syrup

AVOCADO-TOMATILLO SAUCE

Makes about 1 cup

1 ripe avocado, halved, pitted, and peeled

2 tomatillos, husked and roughly chopped

¼ cup diced white onion

½ serrano chile, stemmed

1 tablespoon water

½ teaspoon kosher salt

Leaves from 2 sprigs cilantro, chopped (optional)

Every taco stand offers some variation on this simple salsa, which is not guacamole, but is a way to add some creaminess and moisture to a taco. It is essential on anything grilled, such as chicken or carne asada, and is often served with carnitas and *al pasto* tacos.

In a food processor, combine the avocado, tomatillos, onion, serrano chile, water, and salt. Pulse until fairly smooth, about 10 pulses, scraping down the bowl as needed. Add the cilantro (if using), then pulse a couple of times to combine. Transfer to a bowl, then taste and adjust the seasoning with salt if needed.

The salsa will keep well for 24 hours, covered and refrigerated.

GUACAMOLE

Makes about 2 cups

2 large ripe Hass avocados, halved, pitted, peeled, and cut into 1-inch cubes

2 tablespoons fresh lime juice

1 teaspoon kosher salt

2 teaspoons minced serrano chile

2 tablespoons minced white onion

1 Roma tomato, seeded and diced

Guacamole must always be mashed by hand and should never made in a food processor or blender! Processing makes the avocado bitter. A little chunky texture is desirable.

Place the avocado in a small bowl, then stir in the lime juice and salt. Add the serrano chile, onion, and tomato and mash with a fork until combined but fairly chunky.

Serve right away. To store leftovers, press plastic wrap directly against the surface and refrigerate for up to 24 hours.

TACO SLAW

Colorful, crunchy, drippy, and creamy slaw is a fun change from the expected lettuce or plain shredded cabbage commonly served on tacos. I particularly like this on seafood, carnitas, or anything saucy. Adjust the amount of sugar, vinegar, and chile heat to best complement the taco filling underneath.

_____

In a small bowl, whisk together the mayonnaise, lemon juice, lime juice, vinegar, salt, and sugar (add to taste) until well combined.

In a bowl, combine the green cabbage, red cabbage, carrot, green onions, radishes (if using), cilantro, serrano chiles (add to taste), and pepitas (if using). Add the mayonnaise mixture and toss until thoroughly mixed. Serve right away or cover and refrigerate for up to 2 days.

Makes about 3 cups

½ cup mayonnaise

1 tablespoon fresh lemon juice

1 tablespoon fresh lime juice

2 teaspoons cider vinegar

½ teaspoon kosher salt

1 to 2 teaspoons sugar

2 cups finely shredded green cabbage

1 cup finely shredded red cabbage

½ cup peeled and shredded carrot

2 green onions, green parts only, thinly sliced

⅓ cup sliced radishes (optional)

½ cup roughly chopped fresh cilantro leaves

1 or 2 serrano chiles, stemmed and minced

½ cup toasted pepitas (shelled pumpkin seeds, optional)

SALSA RANCHERA

Makes 4 cups

1 tablespoon olive oil

1 small white or yellow onion, diced

3 large cloves garlic, minced

2 Anaheim chiles, stemmed, seeded, and diced

1 jalapeño chile, minced

1½ teaspoons ground cumin

1 teaspoon kosher salt

1 teaspoon freshly ground black pepper

One 14½-ounce can diced fire-roasted tomatoes, pureed in the blender with their liquid

2 Roma tomatoes, cored, seeded, and diced

Ranchera sauce cooks up fast—in less than 10 minutes—in the Instant Pot. The Anaheim chiles and fire-roasted tomatoes give the chunky sauce some heat, while the Roma tomatoes give it a fresh taste. Although ranchera is best known as the star player in huevos rancheros, it's also great over a burrito (see page 117) or enchilada (see page 55).

Press **Sauté—normal/medium** on the Instant Pot and heat the oil. Add the onion, garlic, Anaheim chiles, and jalapeño and cook, stirring occasionally, for about 2 minutes, until slightly softened. Add the cumin, salt, and pepper and cook, stirring, for about 2 minutes more, until just softened. Stir in the pureed tomatoes, then press **Cancel**.

Secure the lid and set the Pressure Release to **Sealing**. Press **Pressure Cook**, then set the cooking time for 1 minute.

When the cooking program is complete, press **Cancel**. Perform a quick pressure release by moving the Pressure Release to **Venting**. Open the pot, then press **Sauté—high** and stir in the diced fresh tomatoes. Bring to a simmer and cook, stirring occasionally, for 3 to 5 minutes, until thickened.

Serve right away, or transfer to a container and let cool to room temperature, then cover and refrigerate for up to 3 days.

CHIPOTLE AND GARLIC SALSA

This moderately spicy salsa, made in a food processor, is great on tacos, but you'll wind up using it on everything from oven fries to scrambled eggs. This recipe can easily be doubled or quadrupled. Just be sure to adjust the seasoning—the sauce should be very flavorful.

In a small food processor, combine the garlic and chipotle chiles. Pulse until finely chopped, then process until smooth, scraping down the bowl as needed. Add the mayonnaise, lime juice, and salt, then process until well combined, scraping down the bowl as needed.

Cover and refrigerate for up to 3 days.

Makes ¾ cup

1 large garlic clove, peeled
2 chipotle chiles in adobo sauce
½ cup mayonnaise
1 teaspoon fresh lime juice
½ teaspoon kosher salt

UNO-DOS-TRES SHREDDED CHICKEN AND BROTH

Makes 3 cups shredded chicken and 8 cups broth

1 Roma tomato

½ large white onion, root end intact, peeled

1 California chile, stemmed and seeded

1 tablespoon vegetable oil

2½ pounds boneless, skinless chicken thighs

1 bay leaf

1 teaspoon black peppercorns

1 whole clove

1 allspice berry

½ teaspoon dried Mexican oregano or marjoram

½ teaspoon cumin seeds

½ teaspoon coriander seeds (optional)

¼ teaspoon aniseeds (optional)

8 cups water

2 teaspoons kosher salt

½ head garlic, cut in half horizontally

1 small carrot, peeled and sliced

½ celery stalk, twisted to crush

2 sprigs flat-leaf parsley or cilantro, crushed

This quick recipe is a twofer: it yields plenty of shredded chicken for tacos, enchiladas, tamales, and burritos, as well as a richly flavored broth. You can use the broth as a base for any number of lovely chicken soups, such as Chicken-Tortilla Soup (page 16). I prefer to use bone-in and skin-on chicken here because the flavor is better. Go easy on the salt, as you may need to reduce the broth in some recipes.

Line the inner pot of the Instant Pot with a sheet of aluminum foil and press **Sauté—high**. Add the tomato and onion and cook, turning as little as possible, for 7 to 10 minutes, until charred on all sides and the tomato is softened. Transfer to a plate, then lightly toast the chile on both sides, about 1 minute. Transfer the chile to the plate, then carefully remove and discard the foil.

Add the oil to the Instant Pot. Working in batches, add the chicken in a single layer and cook for about 5 minutes, until golden brown. Using tongs, flip the chicken and cook for about 2 minutes more, until golden brown on the second side. Transfer to a bowl. Add the bay leaf, peppercorns, clove, allspice, oregano, cumin, coriander (if using), and aniseeds (if using) and cook, stirring constantly, for about 1 minute. Press **Cancel**.

Add the charred tomato to the pot and, using the back of a spoon, crush it to a paste. Pour in the water and add the charred onion, toasted chile, salt, garlic, carrot, celery, and parsley. Using a wooden spoon, scrape up any browned bits on the bottom of the pot. Secure the lid and set the Pressure Release to **Sealing**. Press **Meat/Stew**, then set the cooking time for 15 minutes.

When the cooking program is complete, press **Cancel**. Perform a quick pressure release by moving the Pressure Release to **Venting**. Open the pot and let stand for at least 30 minutes.

Transfer the chicken to a plate. When cool enough to handle, remove and discard the skin and bones and shred the meat into bite-size pieces. Transfer to a container for storage. Set a wire-mesh strainer over a large bowl. Wearing heat-resistant mitts if needed, lift the inner pot out of the Instant Pot housing and pour the broth into the strainer. Discard the solids in the strainer.

Spoon about ½ cup of the broth over the chicken to keep the meat moist, then cover and refrigerate for up to 2 days. The broth can be refrigerated in an airtight container for up to 3 days or frozen for up to 3 months.

UNO-DOS-TRES SHREDDED BEEF AND BROTH

Makes about 3 cups
shredded beef and
about 7 cups broth

1 tablespoon vegetable oil

2 pounds beef top round
or stew meat, untrimmed,
cut into 2-inch cubes

1½ pounds beef shank or
beef soup bones

1 large white onion, cut into
quarters

2 Roma tomatoes, whole

1 carrot, peeled and cut
crosswise into 4 pieces

6 garlic cloves, peeled

½ jalapeño chile, stemmed
and seeded

2 bay leaves

2 teaspoons black
peppercorns

2 allspice berries

1 whole clove

2 sprigs epazote or flat-leaf
parsley (optional)

6 cups water

1 teaspoon kosher salt

Like Uno-Dos-Tres Chicken (page 154), this simple recipe yields a bounty of tender shredded meat (for tacos, *machaca*, enchiladas, and burritos) and a flavorful broth for use in soups or *guisados*. For the best flavor and color, brown the beef and vegetables well. If you can get fresh epazote (see page 12), it adds an interesting herbal note.

In a heavy-bottomed large skillet, heat the oil over medium-high heat. Working in batches, add the beef in a single layer and cook until well browned on all sides, about 4 minutes per side. Transfer the beef cubes to the Instant Pot as they are done. When there is enough room in the pan, add the beef shank and cook until well browned on both sides, about 5 minutes per side. Transfer the shank to the Instant Pot.

Add the onion quarters and the tomatoes to the skillet and cook, turning only once or twice, for about 5 minutes, until soft. Transfer to the Instant Pot.

Add the carrot, garlic, jalapeño, bay, peppercorns, allspice, clove, and epazote (if using) to the skillet, and cook, stirring occasionally, about 5 minutes, until the garlic is light golden brown and the spices are fragrant. Pour in 2 cups of the water and, using a wooden spoon, scrape up any browned bits on the bottom of the pan.

Pour the mixture into the Instant Pot. Add the remaining 4 cups water and the salt to the pot.

Secure the lid and set the Pressure Release to **Sealing**. Press **Pressure Cook**, then set the cooking time for 25 minutes.

When the cooking program is complete, press **Cancel**. Perform a quick pressure release by moving the Pressure Release to **Venting**. Open the pot and let cool for 1 hour.

Using tongs, transfer the meat to a plate. Remove any meat from the shank and discard the bones. Set a wire-mesh strainer over a large bowl. Lift the inner pot out of the Instant Pot housing and pour the broth into the strainer. Discard the solids in the strainer.

Spoon about ½ cup of the broth over the meat to keep it moist, then cover and refrigerate for up to 2 days. The broth can be refrigerated in an airtight container for up to 3 days or frozen for up to 3 months.

VARIATION

Use ½ cup red wine, beer, or Coca-Cola in place of ½ cup of the water added to the skillet.

CORN TORTILLAS

Makes eighteen
5-inch tortillas

3 cups masa harina (see Note)

2 teaspoons kosher salt

2 cups lukewarm water, plus more, if needed

1 tablespoon vegetable oil

Nothing beats fresh tortillas, especially when they're handmade and cooked on your own griddle. With a little practice, you'll be a pro.

In a large bowl, combine the masa harina, salt, water, and oil. Using a wooden spoon or your hand, mix thoroughly until the mixture forms a smooth, damp dough that does not stick to your hands. If the dough feels too dry, add more water 1 tablespoon at a time, working it in with your hands. The perfect consistency is like Play-Doh.

Divide the dough into 18 evenly sized portions. Using your hands, roll each portion into a ball. Cover the balls with a clean kitchen towel to prevent them from drying out.

Heat a heavy griddle or large, heavy skillet over high heat. Line a tortilla press with a square cut from a heavy plastic bag. With your hands, slightly flatten one dough ball, place on the tortilla press, then cover with a second plastic square. Close the press and apply pressure until the dough forms a 5-inch round about ⅛ inch thick.

Open the press. Holding the tortilla still in the liner in one hand, peel off the top layer of plastic; reserve the plastic. Flip the tortilla onto the palm of your other hand, then peel off the other layer of plastic and reserve. Turn the tortilla onto the hot griddle and cook for about 2 minutes, or until the bottom has a few brown spots and the top begins to look dry. Using a spatula, flip the tortilla and cook the second side for 1 to 2 minutes, until the tortilla is firm. Transfer the tortilla to a cloth-lined basket (or wrap in foil) to keep warm. Repeat with the remaining dough balls, reusing the plastic squares and stacking the tortillas as they are done.

Serve the tortillas while warm, wrapped in a clean cloth or aluminum foil. Leftover tortillas can be wrapped tightly in plastic wrap and refrigerated for up to 24 hours. Reheat in a dry skillet over medium heat for about 1 minute per side, until softened and flexible, though reheated tortillas will never be as soft as ones that are freshly made.

NOTE I prefer the taste and texture of tortillas made with Maseca brand masa harina.

VARIATION

For Green Tortillas, in a food processor, pulse 3 jalapeño chiles, stemmed and seeded, until finely chopped; transfer to large bowl. Add the leaves from 1 bunch cilantro, roughly chopped; 1 garlic clove, peeled; and 2 teaspoons kosher salt to the food processor and pulse until the cilantro and garlic are finely chopped, about 10 pulses. Add 1 cup water, then process for about 10 seconds, until a smooth puree forms. Transfer the mixture to the bowl with the jalapeños, then stir in an additional 1 cup water and ⅓ cup vegetable oil.

Add 3 cups masa harina to the bowl and mix with a wooden spoon or your hand until the mixture forms a smooth, damp dough that does not stick to your hands. If the dough feels too dry, add more water 1 tablespoon at a time, working it in with your hands. The perfect consistency is like Play-Doh.

Proceed to shape, cook, and serve the tortillas as directed for Corn Tortillas.

chapter 7

DESSERTS

FLAN

Serves 6 to 8

½ cup sugar

5 large eggs

One 12-ounce can condensed milk

One 14-ounce can sweetened condensed milk

¼ cup cream cheese, at room temperature

1 teaspoon vanilla extract

¼ teaspoon kosher salt

Fresh berries for serving

Whipped cream for serving (optional)

Flan can be tricky to make in a conventional oven, but the Instant Pot cooks it perfectly—and fast. My recipe contains a bit of cream cheese for extra smoothness and richness, and it makes its own sauce as it sits in the refrigerator. I like the drama of serving one large flan on a platter, surrounded by fresh berries.

Grease a 7-inch round cake pan with vegetable oil.

Add the sugar to a small saucepan, then set pan over medium-low heat. Cook the sugar, stirring occasionally with a silicone spatula once it begins to melt, until dark golden brown, 3 to 5 minutes. Very carefully pour the caramel into the prepared pan and, using heat-resistant mitts, swirl the pan to evenly coat the bottom.

In a blender, combine the eggs, condensed milk, evaporated milk, cream cheese, vanilla, and salt. Blend until very smooth, then let stand for 5 minutes. Using a spoon, skim off and discard any foam on the surface. Pour the mixture into the caramel-lined cake pan and cover with aluminum foil.

Pour 2 cups water into the Instant Pot. Place the covered pan on a long-handled wire rack. Holding the handles of the rack, lower it into the pot.

Secure the lid and set the Pressure Release to **Sealing**. Press **Pressure Cook**, then set the cooking time for 15 minutes.

When the cooking program is complete, press **Cancel**. Perform a quick pressure release by moving the Pressure Release to **Venting**. Open the pot and, wearing heat-resistant mitts, grab the handles of the rack and lift it out of the pot. Carefully remove the foil from the pan; the center of the flan will still be a little jiggly.

CONTINUED

Dip the blade of a paring knife in water and run it around the edges of the flan to loosen it from the pan. Let cool for 20 minutes. Cover loosely with plastic wrap and refrigerate for at least 8 hours or up to overnight.

To serve, invert a serving platter over the flan, then, holding the cake pan and plate together, quickly turn them both over. Lift off the pan. Surround the flan with fresh berries and pass the whipped cream (if using) on the side.

VARIATION

For, Dulce de Leche Flan, substitute one 14-ounce can Dulce de Leche (following) for the sweetened condensed milk.

DULCE DE LECHE

One 14-ounce can sweetened condensed milk, unopened, label removed

I admit I was nervous the first time I made dulce de leche, the creamy, milky caramel popular in so many Latin American countries. The idea of putting a sealed can into a pressure cooker seemed risky, but the results were spectacular! Remember, the can must be immersed in the water and must not touch the sides and bottom of the pot. Do not use a can with any dents or punctures and make sure to remove the label from the can before cooking.

Place the long-handled wire rack in the Instant Pot, then set the can of sweetened condensed milk on the rack. Pour in water to fill to the 4-liter mark on the inner pot; the can should be fully submerged and must not be touching the sides of the inner pot. Secure the lid and set the Pressure Release to **Sealing**. Press **Pressure Cook** and set the cooking time for 15 minutes.

When the cooking program is complete, press **Cancel**. Let the pressure release naturally for at least 4 hours; do not open the pot before 4 hours have elapsed and do not move the Instant Pot during this time.

Open the pot and remove the can. Refrigerate the can overnight before opening.

USES FOR DULCE DE LECHE

- Thin it with milk—or with heavy cream, *reposado* tequila, and vanilla—to make a sauce to drizzle over any dessert.
- Sandwich it between 2 butter cookies.
- Place a spoonful in the bottom of a serving of Arroz con Leche (facing page).
- Eat it off a spoon, standing in front of the refrigerator.

ARROZ CON LECHE

This simple dessert—a pudding made from white rice, cream, milk, and sugar—begs for embellishment in the form of fresh fruit; I love it with sliced strawberries. The pudding sets up firm and creamy after cooling for about an hour. Almond or soy milk may be substituted if you avoid dairy products.

In a 7-inch-round 1½-quart soufflé dish or a 7-cup round heatproof glass container, combine the rice, sugar, cream, 1½ cups of the milk, the butter, cinnamon stick, and salt. Stir until the sugar has dissolved.

Pour 1½ cups water into the Instant Pot. Cover the dish with aluminum foil. Place the dish on a long-handled wire rack. Holding the handles of the rack, lower it into the pot.

Secure the lid and set the Pressure Release to **Sealing**. Press **Pressure Cook**, then set the cooking time for 15 minutes.

When the cooking program is complete, press **Cancel**. Perform a quick pressure release by moving the Pressure Release to **Venting**. Open the pot and stir the rice pudding, breaking up any clumps. Secure the lid once again and set the Pressure Release handle to **Sealing**. Press **Pressure Cook**, then set the cooking time for 10 minutes.

When the cooking program is complete, press **Cancel**. Let the pressure release naturally for 10 minutes, then move the Pressure Release to **Venting** to release any remaining steam. Open the pot and, wearing heat-resistant mitts, grab the handles of the rack and lift it out of the pot. Carefully remove the foil from the dish. Stir in the remaining ½ cup milk, the vanilla, and dried fruit

CONTINUED

Serves 4 to 6

¾ cup short-grain white rice, rinsed and drained

¼ cup sugar

½ cup heavy cream

2 cups whole milk, plus more if needed

½ teaspoon salted butter, melted

One 3-inch piece cinnamon stick

⅛ teaspoon kosher salt

½ teaspoon vanilla extract

¼ cup dried fruit, such as raisins, cranberries, diced apricots, or diced plums (optional)

Sliced fresh strawberries, fresh raspberries, or fresh blackberries for serving (if using). The pudding will be soupy, but it will thicken as it cools. If you like it softer, stir in a bit more milk.

Let cool for at least 5 minutes, then serve the pudding warm or at room temperature, topped with berries. It is also delicious chilled.

NOTES Add a 2-inch-long strip of lemon zest with the cinnamon stick.

Soak the dried fruit in 2 tablespoons fresh lemon or orange juice, red wine, tequila, or Grand Marnier for at least 20 minutes, then drain and use as directed.

Reduce the sugar to 2 tablespoons and dust the top with crushed piloncillo (see page 12) before serving. Serve the rice pudding with dollops of whipped cream and sprinkled with toasted nuts.

Just before serving, sprinkle the pudding with ¼ cup sweetened shredded dried coconut, toasted, or ¼ cup coarsely grated Mexican chocolate (see page 10).

Place a spoonful of Dulce de Leche (page 164) into each serving bowl before spooning in the rice pudding.

CHOCOLATE TAMALES

Each rich, fudgy chocolate brownie, stuffed with cream cheese and pecans, bakes inside a corn husk in the Instant Pot. This fun dessert may be eaten warm from the cooker or (my preference) chilled. As with anything chocolate, the better the chocolate, the better the brownie. Check the master tamale recipe (page 94) for tips on folding and tying tamales.

In a heatproof bowl set over a saucepan containing about 1 inch of simmering water, melt the butter. Add the chocolate and stir with a silicone spatula until melted. Stir in the instant coffee and vanilla. Remove the bowl from the saucepan and set aside.

In a bowl, using a handheld mixer, beat the eggs and sugar on medium speed for 5 to 7 minutes, until pale and fluffy. Add about ½ cup of the melted chocolate to the eggs and beat to combine. Add this mixture to the remaining melted chocolate and fold with the spatula until well combined, then fold in the flour until no streaks remain. Cover the bowl and refrigerate for 1 hour.

Cut the cream cheese into 12 thin slices. Lay a moistened kitchen towel on a work surface. Place a corn husk on the towel with the narrow end facing away from you. Scoop ⅓ cup of the batter onto the center of the husk, then, using a teaspoon, spread into an even layer, leaving a 1-inch margin on the sides and a 2-inch margin on the top and bottom. Place a slice of the cream cheese in the very center and scatter 2 tablespoons of the pecans over the batter and cream cheese. Fold in the sides of the husk to enclose the cream cheese, then fold down the top and fold up the bottom. Using thin strips of corn husks, tie to secure the filling. Form additional tamales using 11 of the remaining corn husks, batter, cream cheese, and pecans. You should have 4 to 6 corn husks left over for lining the rack.

CONTINUED

Serves 12

¾ cup unsalted butter

1¼ cups good-quality semisweet chocolate chips

2 teaspoons instant coffee granules

1 tablespoon vanilla extract

4 large eggs

1½ cups sugar

1 cup all-purpose flour

½ cup cold cream cheese

1½ cups chopped pecans

16 to 18 large corn husks, soaked and drained (see How to Prepare Dried Corn Husks, page 97)

Vanilla ice cream for serving

Pour 1½ cups water into the Instant Pot and place the long-handled wire rack in the pot. Lay a sheet of aluminum foil on the rack, then cover with a couple of moistened corn husks. Place the tamales in the pot, standing and shingling them on end.

Secure the lid and set the Pressure Release to **Sealing**. Press **Pressure Cook**, then set the cooking time for 25 minutes.

When the cooking program is complete, press **Cancel**. Perform a quick pressure release by moving the Pressure Release to **Venting**. Open the pot and let rest for 5 minutes.

Using tongs, transfer the tamales to individual plates; they will seem soft at first but firm up quickly as they cool. Serve warm, still tied, with ice cream on the side, or open the packets and top with ice cream.

NOTE For a lighter texture, whisk 1 teaspoon baking powder into the flour before folding the flour into the chocolate-egg mixture.

CHURRO BREAD PUDDING

Serves 6 to 8

BREAD PUDDING
3 day-old churros, cut into 1-inch pieces (about 2 cups)

3 cups cut-up firm white bread, in 1-inch pieces

½ cup granulated sugar

1 tablespoon ground cinnamon

¼ teaspoon kosher salt

2 large eggs

1 tablespoon vanilla extract

1 cup heavy cream

1 cup whole milk

SAUCE
¼ cup firmly packed piloncillo (see page 12) or dark brown sugar

1 tablespoon good-quality orange liqueur

1 teaspoon vanilla extract

¾ cup Mexican crema or sour cream

FOR SERVING
½ cup sliced almonds, toasted

2 tablespoons grated Mexican chocolate (see page 10)

Fresh berries (optional)

Sweet, cinnamony churros are transformed into a warm bread pudding, cooked right in your Instant Pot. Serve warm with a simple sauce spiked with Grand Marnier or Patrón Citrónge and a pinch of grated Mexican chocolate.

To make the bread pudding: In a large bowl, toss the churros and bread with ¼ cup of the granulated sugar, the cinnamon, and salt. In bowl, whisk together the eggs, vanilla, cream, and milk, then pour over the bread mixture. Stir well to combine. Cover and refrigerate for at least 1 hour or up to 1 day, stirring occasionally.

Butter a 1½-quart soufflé dish or a 7-cup round heatproof glass container. Spoon the bread mixture into the prepared dish and pour over any remaining custard mixture. Sprinkle with the remaining granulated sugar. Cover with aluminum foil. Pour 2 cups water into the Instant Pot. Place the covered dish on a long-handled wire rack. Holding the handles of the rack, lower it into the pot.

Secure the lid and set the Pressure Release to **Sealing**. Press **Pressure Cook**, then set the cooking time for 55 minutes. While the pudding cooks, make the sauce: In a bowl, combine the piloncillo, orange liqueur, and vanilla and stir until the piloncillo dissolves. Stir in the crema. Cover and refrigerate until ready to serve.

When the cooking program is complete, press **Cancel**. Perform a quick pressure release by moving Pressure Release to **Venting**. Open the pot and, wearing heat-resistant mitts, grab the handles of the rack and lift it out of the pot. Carefully remove the foil from the dish and let cool for at least 5 minutes.

Serve the bread pudding warm or at room temperature, topped with the almonds, chocolate, and berries (if using). Pass the sauce on the side.

NOTE If day-old churros aren't available, you can use additional bread. Increase the bread to 5 cups, increase the cinnamon to 1 tablespoon plus 1 teaspoon, and add an additional 1 tablespoon sugar to the mix.

UPSIDE-DOWN MANGO-COCONUT CAKE

Serves 6 to 8

CAKE

1 ripe but firm mango, peeled, pitted, and thinly sliced

1¾ cups all-purpose flour

2 teaspoons baking powder

½ teaspoon kosher salt

⅔ cup canned coconut milk

2 tablespoons fresh lime juice

2 teaspoons grated lime zest

6 tablespoons salted butter, at room temperature

1 cup sugar

2 large eggs, beaten

2 teaspoons vanilla extract

COCONUT SYRUP

½ cup canned coconut milk

¼ cup sugar or agave syrup

⅛ teaspoon vanilla extract

⅓ cup sweetened shredded coconut, toasted

Fresh berries for serving

Whipped cream for serving

Tropical flavors of mango, coconut, and lime mingle in this delicious cake, which is like a pound cake finished *tres leches*–style, with a soak of sweetened coconut milk. Mango slices, placed decoratively on the bottom of the pan, emerge on top when the cake is unmolded, for an elegant presentation. But you may opt to dice the fruit and fold it in.

To make the cake: Grease 7-inch round cake pan with vegetable shortening. Arrange the mango slices in concentric circles in the bottom of the pan. Reserve any extras pieces to put on top of the batter.

Sift together the flour, baking powder, and salt into a bowl. In a liquid measuring cup, stir together the coconut milk and lime juice.

In a large bowl, using a handheld mixer, beat together the butter and lime zest on medium speed until combined, then gradually add the sugar. Continue to beat for about 5 minutes, until the mixture is light and fluffy. Add the eggs and vanilla and beat until combined. Reduce the speed to low. Alternate adding the flour mixture (in three additions) and the coconut milk mixture (in two additions), starting and ending with the flour mixture, then mix just until combined.

Carefully spoon the batter into the pan, on top of the mango slices, and spread evenly to the edges. Arrange any remaining mango slices in an even layer on the batter. Cover the pan with aluminum foil.

Pour 2 cups water into the Instant Pot. Place the covered pan on a long-handled wire rack. Holding the handles of the rack, lower it into the pot.

Secure the lid and set the Pressure Release handle to **Sealing**. Press **Pressure Cook**, then set the cooking time for 38 minutes.

While the cake cooks, make the syrup: In a liquid measuring cup, stir together the coconut milk, sugar, and vanilla until the sugar dissolves.

When the cooking program is complete, press **Cancel**. Perform a quick pressure release by moving the Pressure Release to **Venting**. Open the pot and, wearing heat-resistant mitts, grab the handles of the rack and lift it out of the pot. Carefully remove the foil from the pan. Run a paring knife around the edges of the cake to loosen it from the pan. Using a skewer, poke holes all over the hot cake, then pour the syrup evenly over the top. Let cool in the pan for 1 hour.

Invert a serving plate over the cake pan, then, holding the pan and plate together, turn them both over. Lift off the pan and let the cake cool to room temperature. Serve sprinkled with the toasted coconut and topped with berries, and with the whipped cream on the side.

NOTES To add a pop of color, place ⅓ cup dried cranberries or fresh raspberries between the mango slices.

If you like, fold ½ cup sweetened shredded dried coconut, toasted, into the batter just before spooning it into the pan.

BLONDIE CAKE

Serves 8

½ cup salted butter

1 cup firmly packed brown sugar

2 teaspoons vanilla extract

3 large eggs, beaten

1 cup all-purpose flour

1¼ teaspoons baking powder

½ teaspoon kosher salt

¾ cup white chocolate chips

1 cup pecans, roughly chopped

2 tablespoons firmly packed crushed piloncillo (see page 12) or dark brown sugar

NOTES If you like, add ⅓ cup dried cranberries and the grated zest of 1 lemon to the batter in place of the pecans and chocolate.

Instead of using pecans, substitute chopped toasted walnuts, almonds, peanuts, or macadamia nuts or toasted pepitas (shelled pumpkin seeds).

This rich butterscotch cake, studded with white chocolate chips and pecans, can be whipped up in about an hour. When cooked, the blondie will be moist and fudgy inside, and even better the next day. For a more pronounced butterscotch flavor, brown the butter gently, until fragrant, before adding the brown sugar.

Butter a 7-inch round cake pan. In a small saucepan over medium-low heat, melt the butter. Remove from the heat, add the brown sugar and vanilla, and stir until well combined. Add the eggs and stir until incorporated.

Sift together the flour, baking powder, and salt into a bowl. Then, using a rubber spatula, fold the flour mixture into the butter mixture. Stir in the white chocolate chips and ½ cup of the pecans. Transfer the batter to the prepared pan and spread to an even thickness. Sprinkle evenly with the remaining ½ cup pecans, followed by the piloncillo. Cover the pan with aluminum foil.

Pour 2 cups water into the Instant Pot. Place the covered pan on a long-handled wire rack. Holding the handles of the rack, lower it into the pot. Secure the lid and set the Pressure Release to **Sealing**. Press **Cake** or **Pressure Cook**, then set the cooking time for 38 minutes.

When the cooking program is complete, press **Cancel**. Perform a quick pressure release by moving the Pressure Release to **Venting**. Open the pot and, wearing heat-resistant mitts, grab the handles of the rack and lift it out of the pot. Carefully remove the foil from the pan. Run a paring knife around the edges of the cake to loosen it from the pan. Let cool for 20 minutes.

Invert a plate over the cake pan, then, holding the pan and plate together, turn them both over. Lift off the pan, then reinvert the cake onto a serving plate. Let cool completely before serving.

COOKING CHARTS

These time charts provide suggested guidelines. Cooking times can easily be adjusted; even 1 or 2 minutes more or less can make a difference in how a recipe turns out and can help you customize the recipe to your doneness preference. Remember, you may not need to cook for as long as you think. You can always add more cooking time at the end, but you can't subtract it! For a more comprehensive guide, consult the user's manual that came with your Instant Pot.

FOOD SAFETY Always check the *internal* temperature of meat with an instant-read thermometer to make sure the food has cooked to a safe temperature.

Beef 140°F

Chicken and ground beef 165°F

Pork 145°F

Rice, beans, and legumes 135°F

REHEATING When reheating any food, including rice and beans, make sure the internal temperature exceeds 165°F, and do not reheat a second time.

MEAT & POULTRY

In this book, the cooking time and the type of release (quick or natural) used for meat and poultry vary with the recipe. In most of my recipes, however, I like to use a quick release and then let the meat or poultry cool almost completely in its cooking juices before continuing with the recipe. That extra time gives these proteins the chance to absorb their delicious cooking juices, so take the additional minutes into account when planning your serving time. The size of the piece of meat or poultry you're preparing affects the cooking time, too, with smaller pieces cooking faster than larger ones.

Meat	Cooking Time	Cook's Note
Beef, Top Round, boneless	25–30 minutes	lean, may be dry
Beef Chuck, boneless	25–30 minutes	best choice for most recipes
Beef, ground	5–10 minutes	85% lean is best choice
Beef Short Ribs, boneless	25 minutes	choose meaty ribs
Chicken Breast, bone-in	20 minutes	tent with foil during cooking
Chicken Breast, boneless	15 minutes	tent with foil during cooking
Chicken, whole	20 minutes	tent with foil during cooking
Chicken Thigh, bone-in	20 minutes	best flavor
Chicken Thigh, boneless	15 minutes	ease of use
Chorizo	10 minutes	pork or beef
Duck Leg	20–25 minutes	cooking time depends on size
Pork Belly	35 minutes	longer time renders fat
Pork Shoulder, bone-in	20–35 minutes	good for soup or shredding
Pork Shoulder, boneless	25–35 minutes	best for carnitas, pibil
Pork, ground	10 minutes	lean is best choice
Sausage Meat	10–15 minutes	cook chicken sausage longer
Turkey Breast, bone-in	30 minutes	tent with foil during cooking
Turkey Thigh, bone-in	30 minutes	tent with foil during cooking

VEGETABLES

Vegetables cook quickly, so be careful with your timing and always use a quick release. Seasoning your cooking liquid with a bit of salt enhances the flavor.

Vegetable	Cooking Time	Cook's Note
Chiles, dry	5 minutes	speeds up soak time
Chiles, Jalapeño	2 minutes	or any small fresh chile
Corn on the Cob	5–7 minutes	cooking time depends on freshness
Corn Kernels	4 minutes	simmer down if still crunchy
Kale or Collards	1 minute	mature, not "baby"
Kale or Spinach (baby)	0	stir raw into inner pot at end
Mushrooms	1–2 minutes	flavor is in the juices
Nopales (cactus)	2 minutes	should be crisp-tender
Plantains	2–5 minutes	firm-ripe or green
Potatoes, New or Fingerling	6–8 minutes	cooking time depends on size and use
Potatoes, White Rose or Red	8 minutes	peeled or unpeeled
Tomatillos	1–2 minutes	cooking time depends on use
Tomatoes, Roma or Plum	1–2 minutes	cooking time depends on use

BEANS, GRAINS, PASTA

Flavorful beans with creamy centers are at the heart of every Mexican meal. The age of the beans can affect the cooking time, so I recommend that you always soak beans for at least 8 hours or up to overnight before cooking. If you don't have the time to soak them, cook the beans for the longer time, use a quick release, and check one. The center should be moist and not crumbly. If necessary, cook for another 5 to 10 minutes. Rice should always be well rinsed and drained before cooking and allowed to steam and "settle" before serving.

Bean, Grain, Pasta	Cooking Time	Cook's Note
Beans, Black	30–35 minutes	rinse well and soak
Beans, Great Northern	20–30 minutes	rinse well and soak
Beans, Pinto	30–35 minutes	rinse well and soak
Lentils	10–15 minutes	cooking time depends on use
Pasta	8 minutes	cook in flavorful liquid
Quinoa	1 minute	rinse well, do not soak
Rice, Brown long-grain	15 minutes	rinse well, do not soak
Rice, pilaf-style	8–15 minutes	rinse well, do not soak
Rice, White long-grain	Rice cycle	rinse well, do not soak

SALSAS

Cooked salsas are a snap in the Instant Pot, ready literally in a few minutes. Salsas should always be assertively seasoned with concentrated flavors, so add no more than the amount of liquid(s) specified in recipes.

Salsa	Cooking Time	Cook's Note
Dried Chile Salsas	5 minutes	freezes well
Fresh Salsas	1–3 minutes	don't overcook

SWEETS

Many sweets take well to the even, moist heat of the Instant Pot. Most recipes will seem soft when the lid is taken off, but they will firm up as they cool. I have found that the flavor of most sweets improves after a few hours.

Dessert	Cooking Time	Cook's Note
Bread Pudding	55 minutes	use a deep pan
Brownies or Blondies	35–38 minutes	watch cook time
Chocolate Tamales or Cupcakes	25 minutes	will seem soft
Dulce de Leche	15 minutes	quick pantry addition
Flan	15 minutes	best flan ever!
Pound Cake	40 minutes	a firm cake
Rice Pudding	25 minutes	stir once during cooking
White Cake	40 minutes	moist and firm

ACKNOWLEDGMENTS

Great food and beautiful books don't just happen, even with an Instant Pot involved. It takes any number of talented people to make it all come together, and I am truly grateful for everyone who worked on *The Essential Mexican Instant Pot Cookbook*. Many thanks to my dear friend and agent, Carole Bidnick, and to editor Emma Rudolph and designers Kara Plikaitis and Lisa Ferkel at Ten Speed Press. Photographer Erin Scott and her assistant, Nicola Parisi, were a pleasure to work with. Stylist Lillian Kang and her awesome assistant, Veronica Laramie, turned my recipes—just words on a page—into pure, sexy deliciousness. A very special thanks to Hannah Rahill of Ten Speed for the opportunity to turn the slow cooker on its head!

Barry, Annie, and Will Schneider gamely tasted their way through the chaos of yet another book and offered many helpful suggestions. A shout-out goes to my many kitchen families, past and present, for your support of my crazy ideas over the decades and into the future.

Finally, this book is dedicated to my dear friends, Patrick O'Brien, Joe Bodolai, Jerry Huckins, and Glenn Kurbis, and with endless love to my mother, Margaret Rundle MacDonald Aitken, and my stepfather, J. Howard Aitken. Thanks for the good times.

ABOUT THE AUTHOR

Deborah MacDonald Schneider is executive chef and partner of award-winning SOL Mexican Cocina and Solita Tacos & Margaritas, with six locations in California, Arizona, and Colorado. She travels extensively in Baja California and mainland Mexico, and explores her love of Mexican food by working with Mexican cooks, eating, and writing. She has authored *Salsas & Moles*, *The Mexican Slow Cooker*, *Amor y Tacos*, *!Baja! Cooking on the Edge* (a *Food & Wine* magazine Best Cookbook of the Year in 2007), *Cooking with the Seasons at Rancho La Puerta* (a James Beard Award nominee in 2009), *Williams Sonoma Rustic Mexican* and *Williams Sonoma Essentials of Latin Cooking*, as well as articles for national magazines, including *O, The Oprah Magazine*, and *Food & Wine*.

Her Mexican cooking classes Mexican Street Food and Mexican Comfort Food are featured on craftsy.com.

Through her restaurant work and writings, Deborah has been influential in the Southern California farm-to-table movement and in supporting sustainable fisheries in California and Baja. She has mentored many young chefs, and supports community groups and culinary fund-raising efforts. She received her Certified Executive Chef (CEC) ranking in 2001 from the American Culinary Federation.

www.solcocina.com   www.solitatacos.com

INDEX

Ten Speed Press and the Ten Speed Press colophon are registered trademarks of Penguin Random House LLC.

INSTANT POT® and associated logos are owned by Double Insight Inc. and are used under license.

Library of Congress Cataloging-in-Publication Data
Names: Schneider, Deborah, 1955- author.
Title: The essential Mexican Instant Pot cookbook / Deborah Schneider.
Description: California : Ten Speed Press, 2018.
Identifiers: LCCN 2018031333
Subjects: LCSH: Cooking, Mexican. | Electric cooking. | Pressure cooking. | LCGFT: Cookbooks.
Classification: LCC TX716.M4 S357 2018 | DDC 641.5972—dc23 LC record available at https://lccn.loc.gov/2018031333

Hardcover ISBN: 978-0-399-58249-3
eBook ISBN: 978-0-399-58250-9

Printed in the United States of America

Design by Lisa Ferkel
Food styling by Lillian Kang
Prop styling by Glenn Jenkins

10 9 8 7 6 5 4 3 2 1

First Edition